A ROAD MAP FOR SHYMKENT–TASHKENT–KHUJAND ECONOMIC CORRIDOR DEVELOPMENT

JANUARY 2021

Creative Commons Attribution 3.0 IGO license (CC BY 3.0 IGO)

© 2021 Asian Development Bank
6 ADB Avenue, Mandaluyong City, 1550 Metro Manila, Philippines
Tel +63 2 8632 4444; Fax +63 2 8636 2444
www.adb.org

Some rights reserved. Published in 2021.

ISBN 978-92-9262-677-8 (print), 978-92-9262-678-5 (electronic); 978-92-9262-679-2 (ebook)
Publication Stock No. TCS210013-2
DOI: http://dx.doi.org/10.22617/TCS210013-2

The views expressed in this publication are those of the authors and do not necessarily reflect the views and policies of the Asian Development Bank (ADB) or its Board of Governors or the governments they represent.

ADB does not guarantee the accuracy of the data included in this publication and accepts no responsibility for any consequence of their use. The mention of specific companies or products of manufacturers does not imply that they are endorsed or recommended by ADB in preference to others of a similar nature that are not mentioned.

By making any designation of or reference to a particular territory or geographic area, or by using the term "country" in this document, ADB does not intend to make any judgments as to the legal or other status of any territory or area.

This work is available under the Creative Commons Attribution 3.0 IGO license (CC BY 3.0 IGO) https://creativecommons.org/licenses/by/3.0/igo/. By using the content of this publication, you agree to be bound by the terms of this license. For attribution, translations, adaptations, and permissions, please read the provisions and terms of use at https://www.adb.org/terms-use#openaccess.

This CC license does not apply to non-ADB copyright materials in this publication. If the material is attributed to another source, please contact the copyright owner or publisher of that source for permission to reproduce it. ADB cannot be held liable for any claims that arise as a result of your use of the material.

Please contact pubsmarketing@adb.org if you have questions or comments with respect to content, or if you wish to obtain copyright permission for your intended use that does not fall within these terms, or for permission to use the ADB logo.

Corrigenda to ADB publications may be found at http://www.adb.org/publications/corrigenda.

Notes:
In this publication, "$" refers to United States dollars.

ADB recognizes "China" as the People's Republic of China.

Cover design by Principe Nicdao.

On the cover: Features representing main sectors and areas (transport connectivity, agriculture value chain, sanitary and phytosanitary measures, tourism) for the Shymkent-Tashkent-Khujand Economic Corridor development (photos from the ADB Photo Library).

Contents

Tables, Figures, and Boxes

Figures

Boxes

Acknowledgments

This study was undertaken on behalf of the Central Asia Regional Economic Cooperation (CAREC) Secretariat of the Asian Development Bank (ADB) under the ADB technical assistance (TA) 9630: Assessing Economic Corridor Development Potential among Kazakhstan, Uzbekistan, and Tajikistan. Safdar Parvez, director of the Regional Cooperation and Operations Coordination Division (CWRC) of the Central and West Asia Department of ADB provided overall guidance; and Xinglan Hu, principal regional cooperation specialist of CWRC managed the TA project. Irene De Roma, programs officer, and Maria Cecilia Sison, operations assistant, CWRC, supported the TA implementation including organizing the TA inception missions, regional consultation workshops, and the publication of this report. The TA team also included international and national consultants: Bahodir Ganiev (lead author of the report), Aradhna Aggarwal, Patricia Georgina Gonzales, Umida Haknazar, Roman Mogilevskii, Shuhrat Nurubloev, and Sergey Solodovnik. Government agencies, business communities, and development partners in Kazakhstan, Uzbekistan, and Tajikistan provided data and inputs to this report.

Guntur Sugiyarto, principal economist; Oleg Samukhin, senior transport specialist; Kristian Rosbach, economist (Regional Cooperation); Dorothea Lazaro, regional cooperation specialist; and Carmen Maria Garcia Perez, regional cooperation specialist of ADB, conducted peer reviews on the draft report.

The TA team expresses its appreciation to Guldana Sadykova, Ganjina Fazilova, and Rovshan Mamurov, CAREC Regional Cooperation Coordinator for Kazakhstan, Tajikistan, and Uzbekistan respectively, for their support in the implementation of the TA, including coordinating with the multi-stakeholders, organizing the inception missions and regional consultation workshops, and facilitating field studies in the three countries. The TA team thanks ADB-based national consultants Jennifer Lapis and Alzeus Alzate for their support in organizing TA-related workshops.

The TA team is grateful to ADB staff at headquarters and at the resident missions in Kazakhstan, Uzbekistan, and Tajikistan for their support and inputs.

The TA and all its activities are funded by the People's Republic of China Poverty Reduction and Regional Cooperation Fund.

Abbreviations

ABEC	Almaty–Bishkek Economic Corridor
ADB	Asian Development Bank
ASEAN	Association of Southeast Asian Nations
ATA	Admission Temporaire/Temporary Admission
BCP	border crossing point
CAREC	Central Asia Regional Economic Cooperation
CATS/ICE	CAREC Advanced Transit System/Information Common Exchange
CBT	community-based tourism
CIC	Cascadia Innovation Corridor
CIS	Commonwealth of Independent States
CMR Convention	Convention on the Contract for the International Carriage of Goods by Road
Codex	Codex Alimentarius Commission
COVID-19	coronavirus disease
CWRC	Regional Cooperation and Operations Coordination Division of the Central and West Asia Department
EAEU	Eurasian Economic Union
eTIR	electronic TIR
EU	European Union
Euromontana	European Association of Mountain Areas
FAO	Food and Agriculture Organization of the United Nations
FDI	foreign direct investment
FEZ	free economic zone
GACC	General Administration of China Customs
GDP	gross domestic product
GFSI	Global Food Safety Initiative
GAP	good agricultural practices
GHP	good hygiene practices
GMS	Great Mekong Subregion
GRP	gross regional product
ha	hectare
HACCP	hazard analysis and critical control points

ICT	information and communication technology
IFOAM	International Federation of Organic Agriculture Movements
IPPC	International Plant Protection Convention
ISO	International Organization for Standardization
ISPM	International Standards for Phytosanitary Measures
ITS	intelligent transport system
JCC	joint customs control
km	kilometer
MCGA	Mongolia General Customs Administration
M&E	monitoring and evaluation
O&M	operation and maintenance
OIE	World Organisation for Animal Health
PPP	public–private partnership
PRC	People's Republic of China
R&D	research and development
RFID	radio-frequency identification
SEZ	special economic zone
SPS	sanitary and phytosanitary
STKEC	Shymkent–Tashkent–Khujand Economic Corridor
TA	technical assistance
TIR	Transports Internationaux Routiers
TNEC	transnational economic corridor
TWG	thematic working group
UCM	unified cargo manifest
UNESCO	United Nations Educational, Scientific and Cultural Organization
UNWTO	United Nations World Tourism Organization
US	United States
WIM	weigh-in-motion
WTO	World Trade Organization

1 Introduction

Country relations among Kazakhstan, Tajikistan, and Uzbekistan have improved markedly over the past several years. Barriers to cross-border movements of goods and people among these countries have been significantly lowered. Tajikistan and Uzbekistan, which had strained relations for about 2 decades, have abolished visa requirements for visits up to 30 days. They have also reopened many border crossing points (BCPs) that were closed in the 1990s. Kazakhstan and Uzbekistan have held a number of Kazakh–Uzbek business forums where contracts worth millions of United States (US) dollars were signed.

As a result, trade and tourist flows among the three countries increased considerably during 2017–2019. Bilateral merchandise trade between Kazakhstan and Uzbekistan rose—from $1.8 billion in 2016 to $4.1 billion in 2019. Bilateral trade between Tajikistan and Uzbekistan expanded—from $81.8 million to $470.6 million—over the same period. The number of citizens of Tajikistan that visited Kazakhstan and Uzbekistan increased 4.4 times between 2016 and 2018, and the number of citizens of Uzbekistan that visited Kazakhstan and Tajikistan more than doubled during the same period.[1]

The coronavirus disease (COVID-19) pandemic caused a temporary setback in regional economic integration in Central Asia. To contain the spread of the disease, Kazakhstan, Tajikistan, and Uzbekistan imposed restrictions on the cross-border movement of people in early 2020. They also imposed various forms of internal lockdown measures. Although all three countries lifted most of their internal lockdown measures during May–August 2020, they are expected to maintain some restrictions on international travels in the near term.

Nonetheless, the governments of Kazakhstan, Tajikistan, and Uzbekistan remain committed to deepening the economic integration of their countries in the medium to long term. They intend to implement joint projects in transport, energy, and other sectors. Kazakhstan and Uzbekistan plan to expand bilateral merchandise trade to $5 billion within the next several years. Similarly, Tajikistan and Uzbekistan aim to boost bilateral merchandise trade to $1 billion in the medium term. The three countries are also keen to collaborate in increasing their exports of goods and services to other countries by facilitating transit trade.

The development of transnational economic corridors (TNECs) can be very useful to Kazakhstan, Tajikistan, and Uzbekistan in deepening their economic integration with each other and the rest of the world. In recent years, the TNEC has emerged as an effective tool for increasing regional economic cooperation and integration and for fostering spatially balanced economic growth and development. One of the operational clusters of the long-term strategic framework for the Central Asia Regional Economic Cooperation (CAREC) Program[2]

---

[1] The figures on bilateral merchandise trade were derived from the International Monetary Fund's Direction of Trade Statistics database. The numbers on cross-border movement of people were derived from data published or provided by the governments of Kazakhstan, Tajikistan, and Uzbekistan.

[2] The CAREC Program is a partnership of 11 countries—Afghanistan, Azerbaijan, the People's Republic of China, Georgia, Kazakhstan, the Kyrgyz Republic, Mongolia, Pakistan, Tajikistan, Turkmenistan, and Uzbekistan—supported by development partners. The CAREC Program aims to foster economic development by promoting regional economic cooperation and integration.

leading to 2030—CAREC 2030 strategy includes economic corridor development along with trade and tourism development.[3]

In October 2018, the Asian Development Bank (ADB) approved a technical assistance (TA) to assess the potential for developing a TNEC among Kazakhstan, Uzbekistan, and Tajikistan, with geographic focus on (i) Shymkent city and Turkestan oblast of Kazakhstan, (ii) Tashkent city and Tashkent oblast of Uzbekistan, and (iii) Sugd oblast (including Khujand city) of Tajikistan.[4] The TA is to support the efforts of the governments of Kazakhstan, Tajikistan, and Uzbekistan to deepen the economic integration of their countries and boost shared prosperity.

This road map for developing the Shymkent–Tashkent–Khujand economic corridor (STKEC) is one of the outputs of the TA. The TA team drafted the road map in close consultation with key stakeholders, including the central and local government agencies; the business communities of Kazakhstan, Tajikistan, and Uzbekistan (henceforth referred to as STKEC countries); and development partners. Major activities include TA inception missions in May, intensive field research work in July and August, and the first regional workshop in December 2019. During the second regional workshop held virtually on 28 August 2020, key stakeholders from the three countries deliberated the road map for the STKEC development with positive feedback. The road map was also regarded as a guiding document in the medium- to long-term development of the STKEC.

---

[3]   Asian Development Bank. 2017. *CAREC 2030: Connecting the Region for Shared and Sustainable Development.* Manila.

[4]   ADB. 2018. *Technical Assistance for Assessing Economic Corridor Development Potential among Kazakhstan, Uzbekistan, and Tajikistan.* Manila.

2 International Experience in Developing Transnational Economic Corridors

An economic corridor—also referred to as a development corridor—can be defined as a geographic area with superior transport connectivity, relatively high population density, and robust economic activity. Typically, it includes several big cities, which serve as the main economic nodes (hubs) of the corridor, and the areas around and between these cities. Not only the big cities, but also secondary towns and rural areas inside an economic corridor benefit from superior transport connectivity and economies of agglomeration. Such economic corridor fosters spatially balanced economic growth and development.

A TNEC—also known as a cross-border or a regional economic corridor—is an economic corridor that spans two or more countries. It is characterized by the seamless movement of goods and people across borders and extensive cross-border trade and investment flows. A TNEC provides the agglomerated economies with the benefits of regional economic cooperation and integration. This combination generates considerable welfare gains through lower transaction costs, more efficient allocation of resources, specialization, economies of scale, knowledge spillovers, and positive network effects, among others. It spurs long-run economic growth by enhancing competition, attracting private investment, and promoting innovation.

Throughout the history of humankind, numerous economic corridors, including TNECs, emerged without government intervention along major roads, rivers, railways, and international trade routes. During the past century, the governments of various countries (e.g., Malaysia and South Africa) established national economic corridors to achieve certain development objectives, such as promoting industrialization and a spatially balanced economic development. National economic corridors, whenever these were established by governments, generally entailed large amounts of public investment in infrastructure, such as roads, railways, power grids, and irrigation infrastructure. In some cases, the governments created special legal, regulatory, and institutional frameworks for the economic corridors to attract private investment and stimulate economic activity.

Since the late 1990s, governments of neighboring countries have increasingly used TNECs as a tool for deepening regional economic cooperation and integration, and for boosting shared prosperity. TNECs are being developed in many parts of the world, including Asia, Africa, Europe, and North America. In most cases, the countries are transforming an existing transnational transport corridor into a TNEC. In other cases, they are establishing one or more cross-border transport corridors as part of TNEC development. To promote cross-border trade and spur economic activity along the TNECs, the countries have implemented (or are implementing) investment projects in various sectors (e.g., transport, tourism, power generation, urban development, and education). In many cases, they have also taken measures—such as simplifying and harmonizing border-crossing procedures—to lower legal, regulatory, and procedural barriers to cross-border movements of people, vehicles, and goods. In some cases, special economic zones (SEZs) were set up within a TNEC to increase cross-border investment flows and develop regional production networks.

2.1   Greater Mekong Subregion Economic Corridors

In 1992, the six countries comprising the Greater Mekong Subregion (GMS)[5] launched—with ADB's assistance—the GMS Economic Cooperation Program to enhance their economic relations. In the years that followed, the GMS countries significantly improved their transport connectivity by developing a number of subregional transport corridors. In 1998, they adopted the economic corridor approach and decided to transform some of the transport corridors into three TNECs—the North–South, East–West, and Southern GMS Economic Corridors (Figure 1). Since then, the development of economic corridors has remained one of the strategic priorities of the GMS Program.

Figure 1: Greater Mekong Subregion Economic Corridors

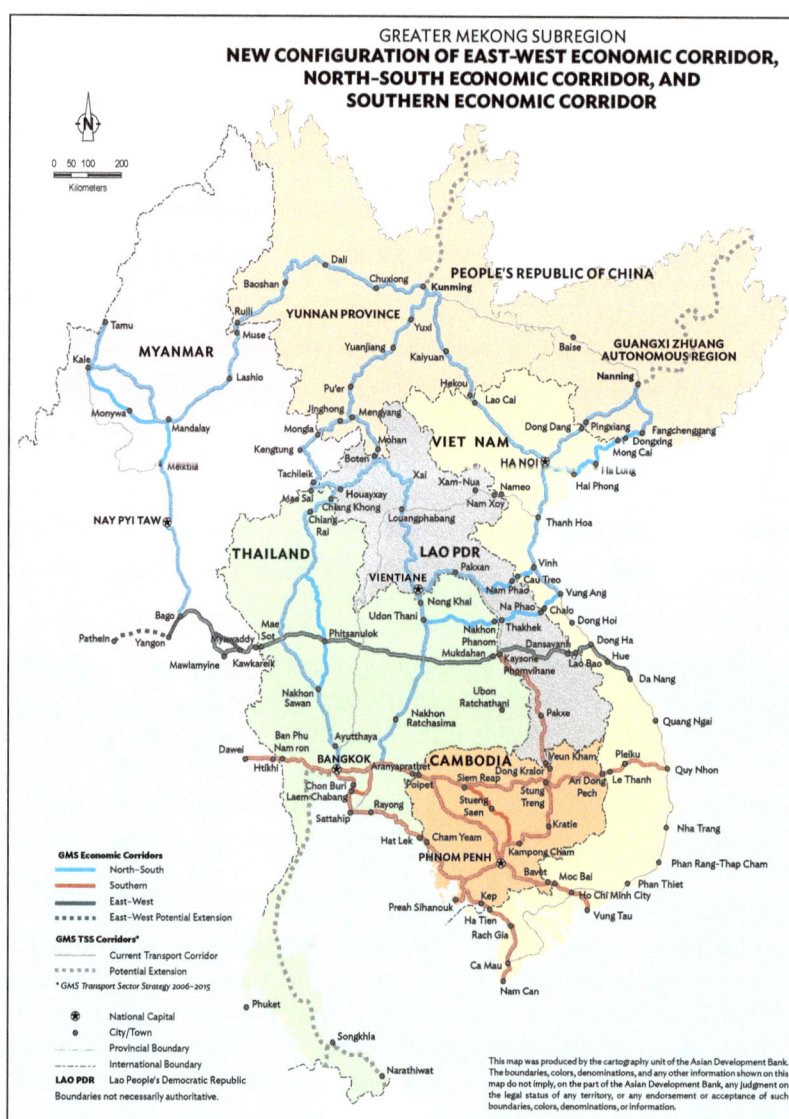

Source: Asian Development Bank.

---

[5]   The GMS is made up of Cambodia, the People's Republic of China (specifically Yunnan Province and Guangxi Zhuang Autonomous Region), the Lao People's Democratic Republic, Myanmar, Thailand, and Viet Nam.

To develop the economic corridors, the GMS countries have implemented—with assistance from ADB and other development partners—several projects in agriculture, energy, environment, health and human resource development, information and communication technology, tourism, transport, trade facilitation, and urban development. They have also signed the GMS Cross-Border Transport Facilitation Agreement, under which vehicles, drivers, goods, and passengers will be allowed to cross the national borders of GMS countries through the GMS road transport system.[6]

Due in part to these GMS economic corridors, cross-border trade, investment flows, and tourist arrivals in the GMS increased considerably during the past decade. Intra-GMS merchandise trade expanded from $26 billion in 2000 to $483 billion in 2017. Bilateral foreign direct investment (FDI) flows among the GMS countries increased from $436 million in 2010 to $1.4 billion in 2017. The number of international visitor arrivals in the GMS rose from 16 million in 2000 to nearly 66 million in 2016.[7]

2.2   Almaty–Bishkek Economic Corridor

The Almaty–Bishkek Economic Corridor (ABEC) covers Almaty city of Kazakhstan, Bishkek city of the Kyrgyz Republic, and the areas around and between these cities (Figure 2). It is a pilot TNEC under the CAREC Program. Its aim is to boost economic activity and raise living standards in Almaty and Bishkek cities and the surrounding areas by (i) reducing travel times; (ii) creating one competitive market for health, education, and tourism services; and (iii) aggregating agricultural produce in wholesale markets to exploit the sector's export potential.

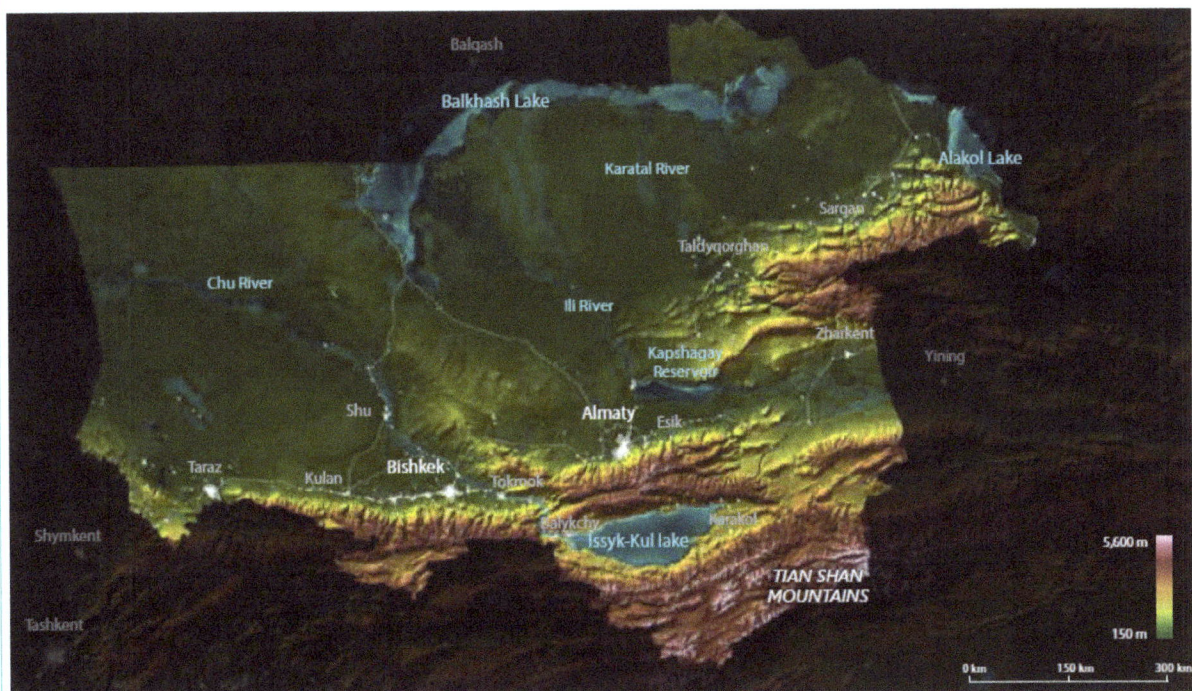

Figure 2: Almaty–Bishkek Economic Corridor

Source: DIVA-GIS. http:www.diva-gis.org/.

---

6   GMS. Cross-Border Transport Agreement. http://www.gms-cbta.org.

7   GMS. Greater Mekong Subregion Program. https://www.greatermekong.org.

In November 2014, the mayors of Almaty and Bishkek cities signed a memorandum of understanding aimed at developing the ABEC. In 2017, the governments of Kazakhstan and the Kyrgyz Republic agreed to oversee the ABEC development through the Intergovernmental Council, chaired by the Prime Ministers of the two countries. The council created the ABEC Subcommittee, a regular official meeting of the two national governments, regional governments, and private sector representatives, cochaired by the Kazakh and Kyrgyz CAREC national focal points. Since then, the ABEC Subcommittee has held meetings regularly. At present, the ABEC continues to progress in the priority sectors and areas, with the ABEC tourism master plan already endorsed by the two countries while investment projects in agriculture, tourism, health, and cross-border connectivity are being developed or planned.

2.3   Maputo Development Corridor

South Africa and Mozambique have been developing the TNEC called the Maputo Development Corridor since the mid-1990s. This corridor includes several landlocked provinces of South Africa and Mozambique's port city of Maputo. It boasts of some of Africa's most effective public–private partnerships (PPPs) in infrastructure development. Trans African Concessions, which operates the N4 toll road connecting Pretoria with Maputo, invested $235 million in the first phase of its build–operate–transfer agreement with the governments of South Africa and Mozambique, and plans to invest another $175 million over the next 20 years. The Maputo Port Development Company, which was given the concession to the Maputo Port in 2003, has had its initial 15-year concession agreement extended to 2033. Between 2003 and 2012, this company invested about $300 million in port infrastructure, equipment, and training and increased the annual throughput capacity of the Maputo port from 3 million tons to 16 million tons. Its 20-year master plan envisions a cumulative investment of $1.7 billion and an increase in the throughput capacity of the port to 48 million tons by 2033.[8] In 2004, eight major private sector players launched the Maputo Corridor Logistics Initiative. Subsequently, more than 100 stakeholders, including public sector entities, have joined the initiative.

2.4   Oresund Region

The Oresund Region is one of the most dynamic and integrated subregions in Europe, with the cities of Copenhagen in Denmark and Malmö in Sweden as its two main hubs. The region generates around 25% of Sweden and Denmark's combined gross domestic product (GDP). Nearly 80% of all jobs are in the service sector, while manufacturing accounts for 20% of employment.

The Oresund Region has developed a structured way to identify and resolve obstacles to cross-border economic integration. Local, regional, and national authorities cooperate through different organizations, including the Greater Copenhagen and Skåne Committee and the Freedom of Movement Council of the Nordic Council of Ministers. In addition, both national governments agreed in 2007 to work together bilaterally to integrate Oresund's labor market.

In 2000, close cooperation between Denmark and Sweden resulted in the opening of the Oresund Bridge, which connects the two countries over the Oresund strait. Since then, Danes and Swedes have crossed the strait in increasing numbers. Among them are some 19,000 cross-border commuters—workers who live in one country and work in the other. They have helped ease the skills shortage in some sectors, generating an additional €6 billion of value-added in the region since the opening of the Oresund Bridge.[9]

---

[8]   B. Mommen. 2012. The Maputo Corridor: Regional Integration that Works. *GREAT Insights*. 1(10). Maastricht: European Centre for Development Policy Management.

[9]   European Commission. 2017. *Overcoming Obstacles in Border Regions: Over the Border for Work, Back in Time for Supper*. Brussels.

However, research indicates that commuter numbers would be much higher if both countries reduced or removed interlinked legal and administrative obstacles to cross-border commuting. Different cross-border organizations in the region are successfully tackling such obstacles. They (i) identify obstacles and discuss potential solutions with the relevant authorities, (ii) provide evidence and information to encourage politicians to remove obstacles, (iii) raise awareness and work with authorities and governments, (iv) monitor the situation to avoid new obstacles, and (v) provide information services for commuters (footnote 9).

2.5   Cascadia Innovation Corridor

The Cascadia Innovation Corridor (CIC) includes Vancouver city of Canada, Seattle and Portland cities of the United States, and the areas surrounding these cities. The development of this TNEC began in 2016, when the local governments of Washington State of the United States and British Columbia province of Canada signed a memorandum of understanding to advance the cross-border innovation economy. Two major business organizations—the Business Council of British Columbia and the Challenge Seattle—supported the development of the CIC.

Under the leadership of the Business Council of British Columbia and Challenge Seattle, a CIC Steering Committee and seven main thematic subcommittees were established. The subcommittees cover the following areas: Life Sciences, Transformative Technologies, Sustainable Agriculture, Transportation, Housing and Connectivity, Best and Diverse Talent, Higher Education Research Excellence, and Efficient People/Goods Movement across the Border.

Projects being implemented or considered within the CIC framework include the following:

- **Vancouver–Seattle–Portland high-speed railway.** This railway will substantially reduce the travel time along the CIC and considerably improve its transport connectivity.

- **Digital Health Initiative.** The British Columbia Cancer Agency and the Fred Hutchinson Cancer Research Center are teaming up to improve rural health care throughout the region.

- **Cascadia Venture Acceleration Network.** This is a network of technology, research, and investment partners from British Columbia, Washington, and Oregon. Its aim is to match technology start-ups with funding and collaboration opportunities, including those across the border.

- **Financial Innovation Network.** Venture capitalists from these three cities are teaming up to increase venture capital funding for start-ups and early-stage companies throughout the CIC.

- **Global Innovation Exchange.** The University of British Columbia is collaborating with the University of Washington and Tsinghau University of the People's Republic of China (PRC) to bring together talented students and faculty to partner with industry in tackling real-world challenges, mostly relating to health care and capacity building projects.

- **Cascadia Urban Analytics Cooperative.** This is another collaboration project of the University of British Columbia and the University of Washington. It utilizes data science and analytics to help solve urban problems.

- **University Collaboration.** Universities throughout Cascadia are teaming up to drive research, innovation, entrepreneurship, workforce development, and economic growth.[10]

---

[10]   F. Cappellano. 2019. *Cross Border Innovation Economies: The Cascadia Innovation Corridor Case.* Bellingham, WA: Border Policy Research Institute.

2.6   Challenges in Developing Transnational Economic Corridors

Economic corridor development involves multisector development and multidisciplinary approaches and is, by nature, a complex process. A TNEC aims to connect different sectors and industries in several countries by applying a coherent spatial economic development approach as if they were in one country. This process involves even more complex and difficult challenges.

Complex and long development process. Unlike a simple road corridor, an economic corridor involves spatial economic planning and development—a multisectoral and multidisciplinary approach requiring careful feasibility studies, multicountry and multisectoral coordination, and pilot testing. It also involves multilevel coordination among national, provincial, and city governments in most cases.

Hard infrastructure gaps and soft infrastructure bottlenecks. While infrastructure connectivity has improved with massive investments in recent decades, developing Asia will need to invest $26 trillion during 2016–2030 or $1.7 trillion per year to bridge the remaining gaps.[11] Regional economic corridor development entails cross-border infrastructure connectivity (e.g., border crossing facilities), which are usually weak links in a given country. Coordination and harmonization in soft infrastructure are also limited, such as customs procedures and trade policies and regulations, which are significant challenges for TNEC development.

Cross-border policy coordination. Countries that are trying to develop an economic corridor are usually at different development stages and with different policy priorities. At the country level, there are often significant differences in tariffs and nontariff measures. At the local level, border provinces usually have their own development agenda and policy preferences. Harmonizing these policies at the country and local levels requires a great deal of coordination and strong political commitment, particularly when cross-border security issues are concerned.

Private sector participation. Private sector participation is a key to the success of economic corridor development in developing businesses and creating employment. However, in most Asian countries, it remains limited due to information asymmetry, weak incentives for investment, and poor access to financing. Lack of effective dialogue with public sector stakeholders is partly responsible for these constraints.

Measuring the impacts of economic corridors. Given the multisector and spatial approach of economic corridor development, developing a comprehensive analytical framework to capture all the benefits of an economic corridor development is very difficult, particularly in the case of TNECs. So far, only a few institutions have developed solid analytical frameworks to comprehensively measure cross-border economic benefits of regional projects. The Asia-Pacific Regional Cooperation and Integration Index (ARCII) and the CAREC Regional Integration Index can potentially be used to monitor and measure the benefits of TNEC development.[12]

---

[11]   ADB. 2017. *Meeting Asia's Infrastructure Needs*. Manila.

[12]   The ARCII is a composite index that measures the degree of regional cooperation and integration in Asia and the Pacific. It comprises six subindexes based on 26 indicators to capture the six dimensions of regional economic cooperation and integration. These are (i) trade and investment, (ii) money and finance, (iii) regional value chains, (iv) infrastructure and connectivity, (v) free movement of people, and (vi) institutional and social integration. The CAREC Regional Integration Index is a variant of the ARCII. It measures the depth and extent of regional economic cooperation and integration among the CAREC countries.

2.7   Lessons for Shymkent–Tashkent–Khujand Economic Corridor Development

International experience in TNEC development offers useful lessons for STKEC development.

Geographic selection and spatial planning. Geographic selectivity is crucial to ensuring that the potentials of economic corridor development are realized. This includes the (i) geographic connections and population size of the area and/or region, (ii) access to regional and international markets, and (iii) the alignment and complementarity of production and trade necessary in achieving increased economic benefits (e.g., scale economy, clustering). Spatial planning is important in efficiently organizing economic activity to attract private investments, particularly in coordinating sectors and areas for joint development (e.g., pooling tourism resources to attract more international tourists). It is also key to improving production value chains, especially in standardizing and consolidating production processes to improve the quality of export products in agriculture and/or horticulture value chains.

Technical analysis and comprehensive investment. An economic corridor builds on and amplifies the underlying economic potential, which can attract private investment. Investment is key to the development of economic corridors. Hence, a sound analysis is needed to identify the economic potential of an economic corridor and the most effective ways to build on the existing economic potential. Such analysis must identify the priority sectors and areas, business opportunities, infrastructure needs, policy and regulatory prerequisites, and financing needs. The success of an economic corridor development cannot be based exclusively on public investment. Private investment also plays a key role in generating employment and fostering economic growth. The public sector should focus on maximizing private investment for every unit of public investment. The two key performance indicators for economic corridor development are (i) the amount of private investment mobilized, and (ii) the number of jobs created.

Harmonizing the policies and regulations. Regional economic corridor encompasses more than one country, thus, it is important to harmonize the policies and regulations—to facilitate and improve the cross-border flows of goods and people and increase trade and tourism. In any given TNEC, the border crossing points (BCPs) are usually the key links between two countries, however, they tend to be weak due to uncoordinated procedures and policies. Thus, policy coordination is essential to the proper functioning of a TNEC, in addition to harmonizing trade policies and trade facilitation measures, which include facilitating transit trade. Joint customs control can be a starting point between two neighboring countries. Integrated border management can be implemented at a later phase, as this is an advanced level of cross-border collaboration.

Stakeholder participation. Given its complex process and multidimensional approach, economic corridor development requires a multistakeholder participation to be successful. Since private sector participation is important, an extensive consultation between the private and public sectors, both upstream and downstream, must be done throughout all planning and implementation stages.

Effective institutional mechanism. As economic corridor development involves multicountry, multisector, and multilevel economic activities, a comprehensive and effective institutional mechanism should ensure the smooth functioning of economic activities, particularly in implementing policies and regional investment projects. This institutional mechanism should have political commitment and authority at the highest level to coordinate with different government agencies at different levels (e.g., national, provincial, and city levels) both within and among countries. A good example is the ABEC, which is supported by an effective institutional mechanism guided by a growing belief in the mutual benefits of developing the corridor.

3 Geographic Focus of Shymkent–Tashkent–Khujand Economic Corridor Development

The proposed geographic focus of STKEC development will be on Shymkent city and Turkestan oblast of Kazakhstan, Tashkent city and Tashkent oblast of Uzbekistan, and Sugd oblast (including Khujand city) of Tajikistan (Figure 3). The geographic coverage can be expanded later to include other cities and/or oblasts of the STKEC countries. STKEC coverage can also be extended to the rest of the Fergana Valley and linked with the ABEC.

Figure 3: Geographic Focus of STKEC Development

STKEC = Shymkent–Tashkent–Khujand Economic Corridor.
Source: Asian Development Bank.

There are many reasons why this geographic area—consisting of Shymkent and Tashkent cities; and Turkestan, Tashkent, and Sugd oblasts (henceforth referred to as the STKEC region)—can become a vibrant TNEC. The reasons include (i) its favorable location and spatial features; (ii) relatively good cross-border transport connectivity and large population size; (iii) robust economic activity; (iv) close historical, cultural, and ethnic ties; and (v) the plethora of opportunities that exist among them for a mutually beneficial cross-border economic cooperation and integration.

Spatial features and transport connectivity. The STKEC region is located at the heart of Central Asia, along several international transport corridors. Four of the six CAREC corridors pass through this region (Figure 4). Turkestan and Tashkent oblasts share a long common border. Tashkent oblast also shares a long common border with Sugd oblast. Although Turkestan and Sugd oblasts do not have a common border, Tashkent oblast serves as a land bridge between them.

Figure 4: STKEC Region and the Central Asia Regional Economic Cooperation Corridors

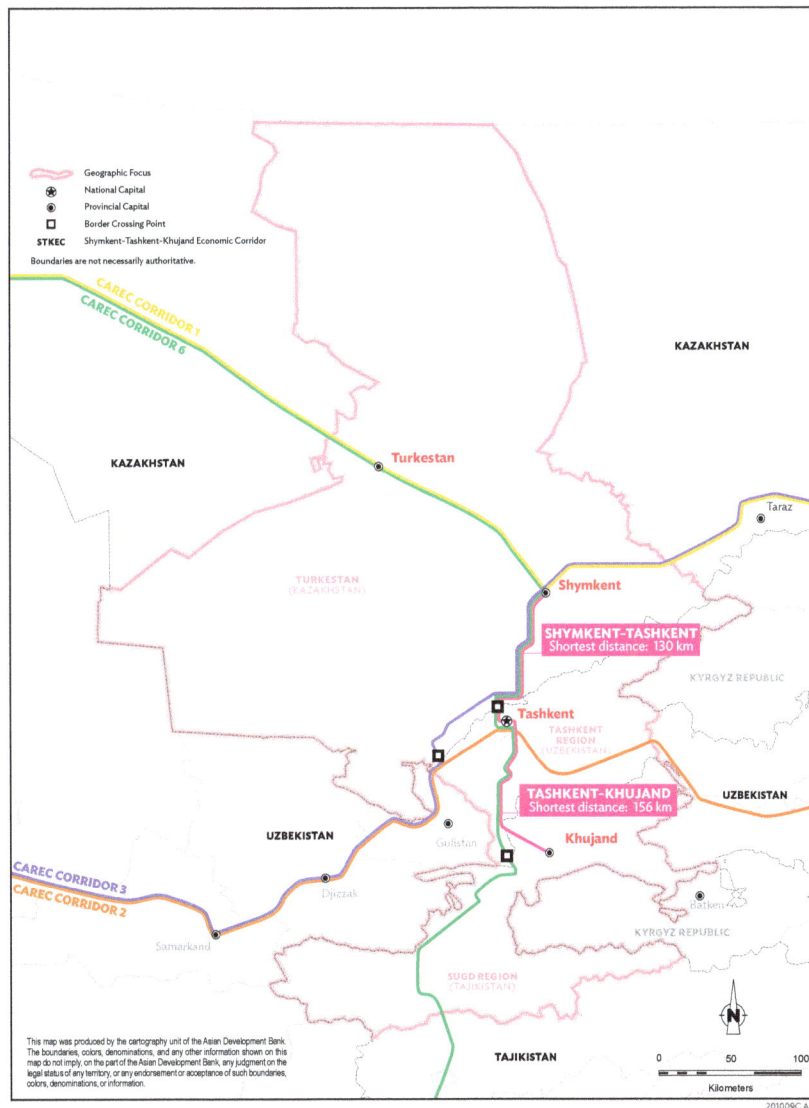

CAREC = Central Asia Regional Economic Cooperation, STKEC = Shymkent–Tashkent–Khujand Economic Corridor.
Source: Asian Development Bank.

Shymkent, Tashkent, and Khujand cities are easily accessible to each other. The shortest road distance between Shymkent and Tashkent cities is 130 kilometers (km), 156 km between Tashkent and Khujand cities, and 280 km between Shymkent and Khujand cities. In addition to roads, railways connect these cities.

Besides Shymkent, Tashkent, and Khujand cities, the STKEC region includes many other clusters of economic activity, such as Angren, Nurafshon, and Turkestan cities.[13] Khujand is not only the administrative center of Sugd oblast, but is also the center of Khujand agglomeration, which includes several secondary towns of the oblast (e.g., Gulison and Istiqlol).

Population. The STKEC region has a large population by Central Asian standards. With a population of more than 1 million people, Shymkent is the third-largest city in Kazakhstan, after Nur-Sultan and Almaty. Tashkent is the largest city not only in Uzbekistan but also in the entire Central Asia. Its official population is over 2.5 million people. Its actual population (including people who are officially residents of other parts of Uzbekistan but live in Tashkent) is much larger. Khujand is the second-largest city in Tajikistan, after Dushanbe. Turkestan, Tashkent, and Sugd oblasts are among the largest provinces of Kazakhstan, Uzbekistan, and Tajikistan, respectively. Turkestan and Sugd oblasts have a sizable ethnic Uzbek minority, while Tashkent oblast has a large ethnic Kazakh minority. At the end of 2018, the official population of the STKEC region was 1.1 million people, which is equal to 15.2% of the total population of Central Asia. The average population density in the region was 69.4 persons per km² (Table 1).

Table 1: Population of STKEC Region, as of end of 2018

	Total Population (million)	Urban Population	Rural Population	Population Density (person per km²)
		(% of total population)		
STKEC Region	**11.1**	**54.2**	**45.8**	**69.4**
Shymkent city	1.0	100.0	0.0	862.5
Turkestan oblast	2.0	19.6	80.4	16.9
Tashkent city	2.5	100.0	0.0	7,496.7
Tashkent oblast	2.9	49.2	50.8	189.4
Sugd oblast	2.7	24.7	75.3	104.7
of which: Khujand city	0.2	100.0	0.0	n.a.
Memorandum Items				
Kazakhstan	18.4	58.2	41.2	6.8
Tajikistan	9.1	26.3	73.7	65.8
Uzbekistan	33.3	50.0	50.0	78.2

km² = square kilometer, n.a. = not available, STKEC = Shymkent–Tashkent–Khujand Economic Corridor.

Sources: Governments of Kazakhstan, Tajikistan, and Uzbekistan; World Bank; and Asian Development Bank estimates.

Gross regional product and density of economic activity. Economic activity is strong in the STKEC region. Real gross regional product (GRP) of the cities and oblasts in the region grew rapidly from 2014 to 2018 (Table 2). In 2018, their combined nominal GRP amounted to $24.5 billion. Density of economic activity, as measured by GRP or GDP per 1,000 km², is on average, higher in the STKEC region than in any of the STKEC countries (Table 3). The density of economic activity is particularly high in Shymkent, Tashkent, and Khujand cities, indicating that these cities can serve as the economic nodes of the region. The service sector generates the largest share of GRP for

---

13   Angren is a town in Tashkent oblast. Nurafshon is the administrative center of Tashkent oblast. Turkestan city is the administrative center of Turkestan oblast.

Shymkent and Tashkent cities and Turkestan and Sugd oblasts. Industry is the largest sector of the Tashkent oblast economy (Figure 5).

Table 2: Growth Rates of Real Gross Regional Product of Cities and Oblasts in STKEC Region, 2014–2018
(%)

	2014	2015	2016	2017	2018
Shymkent city and Turkestan oblast[a]	12.0	4.6	11.2	11.5	12.4
Tashkent city	11.9	10.0	11.5	11.7	8.1
Tashkent oblast	6.4	6.4	6.4	6.4	6.4
Sugd oblast	6.6	6.0	6.9	7.1	6.9
Memorandum Items					
Kazakhstan[b]	4.2	1.2	1.1	4.1	4.1
Tajikistan[b]	6.7	6.0	6.9	7.1	7.3
Uzbekistan[b]	7.2	7.4	6.1	4.5	5.1

STKEC = Shymkent–Tashkent–Khujand Economic Corridor.

[a] The figures for 2014–2017 are for former South–Kazakhstan oblast. The figure for 2018 is for Turkestan oblast only.

[b] The growth rates are for real gross domestic product.

Sources: Governments of Kazakhstan, Tajikistan, and Uzbekistan.

Table 3: Nominal Gross Regional Product and Density of Economic Activity in STKEC Region, 2018

	GRP ($ billion)	GRP per Capita ($)	Density of Economic Activity (GRP in $ per km²)
STKEC Region	24.5	2,213.9	153.6
Shymkent city	6.3	6,250.4	5,390.8
Turkestan oblast	4.8	2,427.2	41.1
Tashkent city	6.6	2,630.2	19,717.7
Tashkent oblast	4.8	1,641.2	310.9
Sugd oblast	2.0	753.8	78.9
Memorandum Items			
Kazakhstan	179.3[a]	9,749.1[b]	66.4[c]
Tajikistan	7.5[a]	824.0[b]	54.2[c]
Uzbekistan	50.5[a]	1,518.1[b]	118.7[c]

GDP = gross domestic product, GRP = gross regional product, km² = square kilometer, STKEC = Shymkent–Tashkent–Khujand Economic Corridor, US = United States.

[a] Nominal GDP in billion US dollars.

[b] Nominal GDP per capita in US dollars.

[c] Nominal GDP in US dollars per km².

Sources: Governments of Kazakhstan, Tajikistan, and Uzbekistan; International Monetary Fund; World Bank; and Asian Development Bank estimates.

Figure 5: Composition of Gross Regional Product of Shymkent and Tashkent Cities and Turkestan, Tashkent, and Sugd Oblasts, 2018
(%)

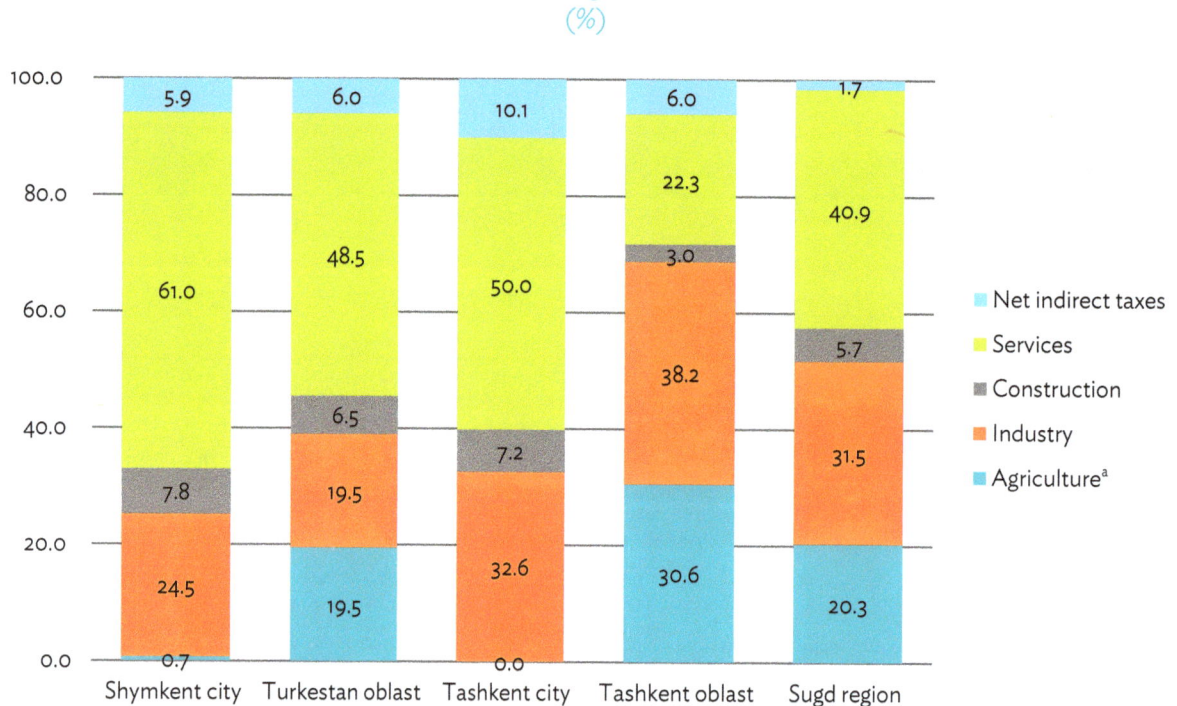

	Shymkent city	Turkestan oblast	Tashkent city	Tashkent oblast	Sugd region
Net indirect taxes	5.9	6.0	10.1	6.0	1.7
Services	61.0	48.5	50.0	22.3	40.9
Construction	7.8	6.5	7.2	3.0	5.7
Industry	24.5	19.5	32.6	38.2	31.5
Agriculture	0.7	19.5	0.0	30.6	20.3

a Includes hunting, forestry, and fishing.

Sources: Statistics Committee of the Ministry of National Economy of the Republic of Kazakhstan; Government of the Republic of Tajikistan; State Committee of the Republic of Uzbekistan on Statistics; and Asian Development Bank estimates.

Intraregional merchandise trade. All three STKEC countries are members of the Free Trade Area of the Commonwealth of Independent States (CIS).[14] As such, they apply no import tariffs on bilateral merchandise trade (with some exceptions). However, trade among the STKEC countries is subject to various nontariff barriers, such as sanitary and phytosanitary (SPS) measures and technical barriers.

While reliable data on cross-border trade flows among the Kazakh, Uzbek, and Tajik parts of the STKEC region are not available, estimates based on indirect statistics indicate that merchandise trade between the Kazakh and Uzbek parts of the region and between the Kazakh and Tajik parts decreased between 2015 and 2018.[15] At the same time, merchandise trade between the Tajik and Uzbek parts increased, albeit from a low base (Table 4). Total intraregional trade in goods declined from $599.1 million in 2015 to $341.5 million in 2018.

---

[14] The other members of the CIS free trade area are Armenia, Belarus, the Kyrgyz Republic, Moldova, the Russian Federation, and Ukraine.

[15] Merchandise trade between the Kazakh and Uzbek parts of the region declined because Uzbekistan reduced its imports of Kazakh wheat and its exports of vegetables and fruits to Kazakhstan. Meanwhile, merchandise trade between the Kazakh and Tajik parts of the region decreased because Tajikistan discontinued importing Kazakh gas and reduced its exports of vegetables and fruits to Kazakhstan.

Table 4: Intraregional Merchandise Trade in the STKEC Region, 2015 and 2018
($ million)

| | Importer | | | | | |
| | Shymkent city and Turkestan oblast | | Tashkent city and Tashkent oblast | | Sugd oblast | |
Exporter	2015	2018	2015	2018	2015	2018
Shymkent city and Turkestan oblast			206.8	136.1	39.2	14.1
Tashkent city and Tashkent oblast	329.3	76.4			1.9	36.4
Sugd oblast	19.6	0.9	2.3	77.5		

STKEC = Shymkent–Tashkent–Khujand Economic Corridor.

Sources: Governments of Kazakhstan, Uzbekistan, and Tajikistan; and Asian Development Bank estimates.

Consequently, cross-border trade flows within the STKEC region remain relatively small. In 2018, only a small fraction of Tashkent city and Tashkent oblast's imports and exports were with the Kazakh and Tajik parts of the STKEC region. Similarly, Shymkent city and Turkestan oblast's merchandise imports and exports comprised only a small proportion of trade with Sugd oblast. Total cross-border trade within the STKEC region accounted only 7.5% of total trade among STKEC countries.

Moreover, cross-border trade within the STKEC region is concentrated in only a small number of goods. The three main traded product groups are (i) zinc ore and concentrate, supplied by the Tajik–Chinese joint venture Gorprom in Sugd oblast to Almalyk mining and metallurgy plant in Tashkent oblast; (ii) vegetables and fruits exported from Tashkent oblast to Kazakh; and (iii) wheat grain and flour exported from Kazakh to the Uzbek part of the region (Figure 6).

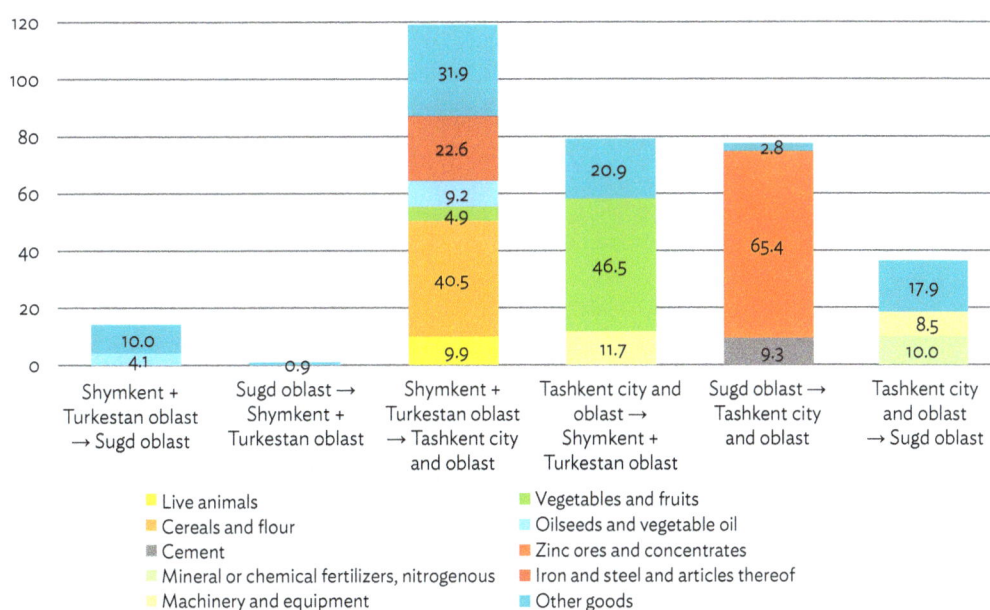

Figure 6: Composition of Cross-Border Trade within STKEC Region, 2018
($ million)

STKEC = Shymkent–Tashkent–Khujand Economic Corridor.

Sources: Statistics Committee of the Ministry of National Economy of the Republic of Kazakhstan, Government of the Republic of Tajikistan, State Committee of the Republic of Uzbekistan on Statistics, and Asian Development Bank estimates.

Transit trade. The STKEC region is a major transit corridor. Shymkent city and Turkestan oblast serve as transit for Uzbekistan and Tajikistan's trade with the non-STKEC parts of Kazakhstan, the Russian Federation, and other countries. They serve as gateways for Uzbekistan, and to a lesser extent, for Tajikistan's exports of fresh and dried fruits and vegetables to the Eurasian Economic Union (EAEU). A large proportion of the PRC's exports to Uzbekistan pass through the Kazakh part of the STKEC region. Likewise, Tashkent city and Tashkent oblast physically bridge Tajikistan's foreign trade. Further, Tashkent city and Sugd oblast serve as gateways for foreign trade in Uzbekistan and Tajikistan, respectively.[16] A substantial percentage of Kazakhstan and the Russian Federation's exports to Afghanistan transits through the STKEC region. The total value of formal transit trade through the region is estimated to be between $20.5 billion and $25.5 billion in 2018,[17] 60–75 times larger than the value of officially recorded intraregional trade in the same year.

Informal trade. Official statistics do not fully capture all the trade flows in Central Asia, including the STKEC region. Close historical and cultural ties between people on different sides of state borders, porous borders between some Central Asian countries, weaknesses in governance, and shuttle trade result in significant informal cross-border flows of goods. Motivation for keeping these flows informal include import tax evasion and attempts to benefit from the preferential trade regime enjoyed by entities based in a neighboring country.

A major type of informal trade in the STKEC region is the reexport of Chinese consumer goods—such as garments, footwear, and electronics—by individuals from Central Asian countries bordering the PRC (Kazakhstan, the Kyrgyz Republic, and Tajikistan) to countries that have no common border with the PRC (e.g., Uzbekistan). There is a gap of several billion US dollars between the PRC-reported value of exports of light industry products from the PRC to Kazakhstan and the Kazakhstan-reported value of imports of these goods to Kazakhstan from the PRC. The difference, most probably, accounts for informal imports of light industry products from the PRC to Kazakhstan. These imports are partly intended for the domestic market of Kazakhstan and partly for reexport to neighboring countries, such as Uzbekistan. The total value of the reexports could be in the order of $0.5 billion–$1.0 billion, with a considerable portion going to Uzbekistan via the border between Turkestan and Tashkent oblasts.[18]

Opportunities for cross-border economic cooperation and integration. The scope for expanding interindustry trade in goods and services within the STKEC region seems to be limited.[19] The composition of merchandise exports of the Kazakh, Uzbek, and Tajik parts of the region overlaps to a considerable extent;[20] and so does the composition of their merchandise imports. Accordingly, the value of the trade complementarity index among the three parts of the STKEC region is low (i.e., 20%–30%).[21]

However, there is a lot of opportunity for expanding intra-industry trade in differentiated goods and services within the STKEC region.[22] This applies to a broad range of goods and services, including food and textile products,

---

[16] In 2018, Tashkent city accounted for 8.5% of Uzbekistan's merchandise exports, and 37.1% of the country's merchandise imports. Sugd oblast accounted for 54.2 % of Tajikistan merchandise exports, and 48.1% of the country's merchandise imports.

[17] The numbers are only for formal transit trade flows carried by road and rail transport. They do not include transit trade flows carried by air and pipeline transport; nor do they include informal transit flows.

[18] More information about international trade in the STKEC region can be found in the companion report, *Assessing the Potential for Trade along the Shymkent–Tashkent–Khujand Economic Corridor.*

[19] Interindustry trade in goods and services are trade in goods and services produced or rendered by different industries.

[20] Data on the composition of services exports of the three parts of the STKEC region are currently unavailable.

[21] The trade complementarity index is a measure of the scope of interindustry trade in goods. Its value ranges from 0% to 100%, with a higher value corresponding to a greater scope of interindustry trade.

[22] Intra-industry trade in differentiated goods and services are produced and rendered by the same industries but have somewhat different characteristics. Like interindustry trade, intra-industry trade fosters economic growth and improves social welfare by enabling producers to achieve economies of scale, enhancing competition among them, and increasing the variety of goods and services available to consumers.

construction materials, chemical products (such as fertilizers and pharmaceuticals), tourism-related services, tertiary health-care services, higher and vocational education services, agricultural extension services, and quality testing and certification services.

There is also a lot of opportunity for expanding exports of goods and service to non-STKEC countries by increasing cross-border economic cooperation and integration within the region. Notably, all three parts of the region can boost transit trade flows and exports of transport and storage services to non-STKEC countries by increasing collaboration in transport and trade facilitation. They can also expand exports of fruits and vegetables to the Russian Federation, the PRC, and other countries by (i) increasing cooperation in transport and trade facilitation, (ii) developing horticulture value chains, (iii) modernizing SPS measures, and (iv) developing food quality certification services. They can attract more tourists from outside the region by developing and marketing regional tourism products, facilitating cross-border movement of people, and collaborating more closely in preventing or containing the spread of communicable diseases, such as COVID-19.

Lowering the barriers to cross-border trade and investment flows within the STKEC region can help STKEC countries develop cost-efficient and reliable regional supply chains for essential goods such as food products, pharmaceuticals, and medical equipment.[23] STKEC countries could also develop manufacturing and boost the export of their manufactured goods.[24] Once STKEC is fully developed, firms based in the region will find it easier to export their products to neighboring countries. By exporting to neighboring countries, many manufacturing firms will gain knowledge and experience that will further enable them to export to other countries. Thus, the STKEC can serve as a testing ground for the export of manufactured goods from STKEC countries to global markets. There are many other areas and forms of cross-border economic cooperation and integration that Shymkent and Tashkent cities and Turkestan, Tashkent and Sugd oblasts can pursue and benefit from within the framework of STKEC development. These include joint projects in research and experimental development (including agricultural research and development [R&D]), exchange of knowledge on plant and animal health protection, new agricultural technologies and urban planning, and coordinated development of and cross-border investments in SEZs and industrial zones.

---

[23]   The COVID-19 pandemic highlighted the importance of the reliability of supply chains, especially for pharmaceuticals, medical equipment, and food products.

[24]   Manufacturing is currently underdeveloped in STKEC countries and primary commodities dominate their merchandise exports.

4 Thematic Focus Areas

Among stakeholders, the broad consensus is that efforts to develop the Shymkent–Tashkent–Khujand Economic Corridor (STKEC) should focus on the following six intertwined thematic areas, where efforts can yield mutually beneficial results relatively quickly:

(i)   improvement of road and railway transport connectivity,

(ii)   modernization of border crossing points (BCPs) and border management,

(iii) development of horticulture value chains,

(iv)   modernization of sanitary and phytosanitary (SPS) measures and development of food quality certification services,

(v)   development of regional tourism, and

(vi)   development of special economic zones (SEZs) and industrial zones.

These six focus areas are consistent with the development priorities of (i) the central governments of Kazakhstan, Tajikistan, and Uzbekistan; (ii) the local governments of Shymkent and Tashkent cities; and (iii) Turkestan, Tashkent, and Sugd oblasts. If needed, the list can be subsequently expanded—by adding other thematic areas, such as urban development and education.

4.1   Improvement of Road and Railway Transport Connectivity

Although transport connectivity in the STKEC region is relatively good, it has many weaknesses. To turn the region into a vibrant transnational economic corridor (TNEC), weaknesses in its transport connectivity need to be eliminated or at least alleviated. Improving road and railway transport connectivity is particularly important. These two modes of transport account for all freight and passenger traffic (including cross-border traffic) within the STKEC region and the bulk of freight traffic between the region and the rest of the world.

Road Transport

Road transport accounts for most of the cargo traffic within the STKEC region. It also accounts for large proportions of outbound and inbound shipments of some goods (such as fresh fruits and vegetables). Within the STKEC region, people travel mainly by road. Hence, improving road transport connectivity is critical to increasing intraregional trade, expanding its exports of fruits and vegetables, and developing tourism in the region.

Road network. The STKEC region has an extensive road network. Most primary and secondary roads in the region, including the roads connecting Shymkent, Tashkent, and Khujand cities, are in good condition. Many of these roads were rehabilitated or upgraded during the past decade—in some cases, with assistance from international financial institutions.[25] Numerous new roadside facilities, such as gas stations and rest areas, were also built.

However, some secondary roads and several tertiary roads still need to be rehabilitated or upgraded. Among these is the Khujand–Asht road, which links Khujand city to the northeastern part of Sugd oblast. There is a need to construct new roads and additional roadside facilities to accommodate the rapidly growing traffic in the region. Many roads need to be built or rehabilitated to improve the transport connectivity of Turkestan city and turn it into a major economic hub.

Section of Khujand-Asht Road which needs upgrade (Source: Asian Development Bank).

The STKEC countries are implementing or planning to implement many road projects in the region. Some of these will potentially improve not only each country's internal connectivity, but also the cross-border transport connectivity among STKEC countries. For instance, Kazakhstan is planning to build new roads in the southern part of Turkestan oblast, which can improve transport connectivity between Turkestan and Tashkent oblasts. By closely coordinating the design and implementation of such projects, STKEC countries can increase the positive impacts of the transport connectivity of the region.

Operation and maintenance of roads. Like in other parts of Central Asia, the operation and maintenance (O&M) of roads in the STKEC region (including those recently rehabilitated) is less than adequate. The reasons include weak traffic management, insufficient funding for the O&M of roads, and in many cases, low quality of maintenance work. Inefficient operation and inadequate maintenance could cause road conditions to deteriorate quickly, especially if traffic continues to grow rapidly.[26]

To keep roads in good condition and ensure road safety, Kazakhstan established 24 fixed vehicle weigh stations on roads and at BCPs. It also deployed 36 mobile weigh stations. Most of the fixed stations and all the mobile stations

---

[25]   For instance, ADB has financed the rehabilitation of a 37-kilometer section of the Shymkent–Tashkent road, which is part of the CAREC Corridor 3. ADB. 2018. *Kazakhstan: CAREC Corridor 3 (Shymkent–Tashkent Section) Road Improvement Project. Completion Report.* Manila.

[26]   ADB. 2019. *CAREC Transport Strategy 2030.* Manila.

employ weigh-in-motion (WIM) devices.[27] Three of these mobile stations are deployed in Turkestan oblast and are used on roads leading to BCPs. While there are no fixed stations with WIM devices in the Kazakh part of the STKEC region, there are fixed stations in the Kazakh side—on road BCPs between Turkestan and Tashkent oblast. The weigh stations aim to ensure that both foreign and domestic vehicles comply with the Kazakh national standards on vehicle weights.

However, the scales have low accuracy and/or are not operated properly in many of the weigh stations, including those in the Kazakh part of the STKEC region. Thus, the stations have not been effective in enforcing Kazakh transport regulations. According to road transport operators, they have fueled corruption and became an obstacle for international shipments coming to, from, or through Kazakhstan. Even trucks transporting goods in sealed cargo compartments often have to undergo weighing in several stations in Kazakhstan and scales in different stations sometimes show significantly different weights for the same cargo. Truck drivers with excessive loads often get clearance by paying bribes to station employees.

Tashkent oblast has 14 fixed road vehicle weigh stations. All of these are located at road BCPs and none of them are equipped with WIM devices. The stations use old equipment with limited capabilities and low accuracies in measuring the axle load of trucks. This creates opportunities for corruption and often enables trucks with excess axle loads to enter Uzbekistan without paying a fine. There are no weigh stations inside Tashkent oblast, although such stations are needed to preserve the roads and enhance road safety.

Sugd oblast has three fixed road vehicle weigh stations. One of these belongs to Innovative Road Solutions—the private company that operates the Dushanbe–Khujand–Chanak road—and uses a relatively modern weighing technology. The other two belong to the Ministry of Transport of Tajikistan and use old technology with low accuracy.

Tajikistan applies the so-called "heat regime" to traffic on some roads, including the Tajik part of the Khujand–Tashkent road—to preserve the roads. Under this regime, trucks with axle loads of more than 6 tons are not allowed to use the roads from 8:00 a.m. to 6:00 p.m. during the months of May to September. According to Tajik entrepreneurs, the "heat regime" is a major impediment to the export of fresh fruits and vegetables from Sugd oblast because it often causes delays in international road shipments.

To keep roads in the STKEC region in good condition, reduce transport costs, and increase exports, the countries need to improve the O&M of roads. They can improve the quality of road maintenance work by introducing performance-based contracts. They can strengthen traffic management and reduce transport costs by establishing, through public–private partnerships (PPPs), intelligent transport systems (ITS) with automated WIM stations.[28] Cross-border collaboration, through knowledge exchange among STKEC countries, can be very useful when introducing performance-based road maintenance contracts and establishing ITS with automated WIM stations.

Road transport standards. A major weakness in road transport connectivity in the STKEC region is the varying transport standards of national roads in STKEC countries. This is most observed in the difference between the Kazakh and Uzbek national standards on truck weights. For most types of trucks, the maximum permissible gross weight is 38 tons in Kazakhstan, while it is 40 tons in Uzbekistan. The maximum permissible axle load is also lower in Kazakhstan than in Uzbekistan for most types of truck axles (Table 5). Hence, Uzbek road transport operators often do not fully load their trucks for shipments going to or through Kazakhstan. Sometimes, their drivers pay a

---

[27]   WIM devices measure and record the gross weight and axle load of a vehicle without the vehicle having to stop. They make the weighing process more efficient by letting vehicles not violating the weight limits to bypass static scales or inspection.

[28]   An ITS is a system where modern information and communication technologies are applied in transport, including traffic management and maintenance of the transport infrastructure.

bribe to Kazakh transport inspectors to avoid the fine for excess axle load. This increases the cost of road shipments from Uzbekistan to Kazakhstan and via Kazakhstan to other countries. Tajikistan's national regulations distinguish between single and dual wheel axle loads, creating ambiguity and often causing disputes between road transport operators and transport police. Thus, if national road transport standards among STKEC countries are harmonized, this would reduce corruption and facilitate international shipments by road from, to, and through the STKEC region.

Table 5: Load Limits for Selected Types of Truck Axles in Kazakhstan and Uzbekistan, as of 1 January 2020
(ton)

Types of Truck Axles	Kazakhstan	Uzbekistan	Tajikistan
Single axle with dual wheels	8.0	10.0	10.0
Trailer or semi-trailer tandem axles with single wheels			
0.5 m < distance between the axles < 1.0 m	11.0	12.0	12.0
1.0 m ≤ distance between the axles < 1.3 m	12.0	14.0	14.0
1.3 m ≤ distance between the axles < 1.8 m	13.2	16.0	16.0
1.8 m ≤ distance between the axles	13.6	17.0	18.0
Trailer or semi-trailer tandem axles with dual wheels			
0.5 m < distance between the axles < 1.0 m	12.0	12.0	12.0
1.0 m ≤ distance between the axles < 1.3 m	13.0	16.0	14.0
1.3 m ≤ distance between the axles < 1.8 m	14.2	17.0	16.0
1.8 m ≤ distance between the axles	14.6	18.0	18.0
Trailer or semi-trailer triple axles with single wheels			
0.5 m < distance between the axles < 1.0 m	15.9	16.5	16.0
1.0 m ≤ distance between the axles < 1.3 m	17.2	19.5	18.5
1.3 m ≤ distance between the axles < 1.8 m	19.7	21.0	20.5
1.8 m ≤ distance between the axles	20.4	24.0	22.5
Trailers and semi-trailers triple axles with dual wheels			
0.5 m < distance between the axles < 1.0 m	17.4	17.5	16.0
1.0 m ≤ distance between the axles < 1.3 m	18.4	21.0	18.5
1.3 m ≤ distance between the axles < 1.8 m	21.2	22.5	20.5
1.8 m ≤ distance between the axles	21.9	26.5	22.5

m = meter.

Sources: Asian Development Bank. 2019. *Uzbekistan: Third CAREC Corridor Road Investment Program—Axle Load Control.* Consultant's report. Manila; Agreement on Weights and Dimensions of Vehicles Undertaking Interstate Shipments by Road in Commonwealth of Independent States Member Countries; and Decree of the Government of Tajikistan #779 dated 29 December 2006 (amended in 2014).

Entry permits and fees for trucks and buses. The 2006 bilateral road transport agreement between Kazakhstan and Uzbekistan stipulates that trucks registered on the territory of one of the parties to the agreement can enter the territory of the other party without a permit. They are also exempt from an entry fee (i.e., road tax). However, Kazakh and Uzbek buses need a permit to enter the territory of the other country, but these are exempt from paying an entry fee.

Also based on the 2006 bilateral transport agreement between Kazakhstan and Tajikistan, Kazakh and Tajik trucks can enter the territory of the other country without a permit and are exempt from an entry fee. Kazakh buses are also exempt from entry fees in Tajikistan and vice versa, however, they need a permit to enter the other country.

The 2018 bilateral road transport agreement between Tajikistan and Uzbekistan stipulates that Tajik trucks and buses need a permit to enter Uzbekistan and are subject to an entry fee. The same applies to Uzbek trucks entering Tajikistan. In practice, there are two types of entry permits. One type can only be used by trucks transporting coal or salt between the two countries. Trucks with this type of permit are exempt from paying the entry fee, while trucks with the other type of permit are subjected to the entry fee. The fee varies from $100 to $200 depending on the gross weight of a truck.

In all three countries, the procedure for obtaining an entry permit for a truck or a bus is cumbersome and time-consuming. There is also a shortage of Kazakh permits for buses and Uzbek permits for trucks in Tajikistan because quotas for these permits are imposed. Although the entry fee that Uzbekistan and Tajikistan levy on each other's trucks was reduced in 2019, it is still too high for some export goods (e.g., construction materials). Hence, entry permits and fees for trucks impede trade between Tajikistan and Uzbekistan, and the transit trade in the STKEC region. The entry permits and fees for buses hinder cross-border movement of people and the development of tourism in the region. Abolishing these entry permits and reducing the entry fees would boost trade and spur tourist flows in the STKEC region.

Digitalizing the road transport services. The degree of transforming transport services, including road transport services, into digital forms is still low in STKEC countries despite recent progress in this area. All three STKEC countries have acceded to the Convention on the Contract for the International Carriage of Goods by Road (CMR Convention), which provides a legal framework for international road haulage.[29] However, none of the STKEC countries have ratified the 2008 protocol to the CMR Convention, which provides a legal framework and standards for the use of electronic means to record the CMR consignment note.[30] The low level of digitalization of road transport services is one of the reasons why the cost of international shipments by road in the STKEC region is relatively high. If STKEC countries decide to ratify the 2008 protocol to the CMR Convention and introduce an electronic CMR consignment note, these will provide an impetus for digitalizing the transport services in the region and help reduce the cost of international shipments by road.

Planned and proposed actions. To improve road transport connectivity in the STKEC region, the following actions are planned or proposed:

(i) Rehabilitate or upgrade the existing roads that are important to the external and/or internal transport connectivity of the STKEC region (e.g., Khujand–Asht road in Khujand oblast).

(ii) Construct new roads (e.g., a Saryagash bypass road in Turkestan oblast and a Chirchik ring road in Tashkent oblast) and additional roadside facilities to accommodate the growing traffic in the region.

(iii) Provide adequate funding for the O&M of roads, especially recently built, rehabilitated, or upgraded roads.

(iv) Introduce performance-based contracts to improve the quality of road maintenance work.

(v) Introduce ITS with automated WIM stations along major highways in the STKEC region to strengthen traffic management and road preservation.

(vi) Prohibit repeated weighing of trucks with sealed load compartments.

(vii) Exempt the shipments of perishable goods from the "heat regime" in Tajikistan.

(viii) Harmonize the STKEC countries' national standards on weights of road vehicles to facilitate international shipments by road.

(ix) Abolish the entry permits for the movement of trucks between Tajikistan and Uzbekistan and for the movement of buses among STKEC countries.

(x) Ratify the 2008 protocol to the CMR Convention and introduce the electronic CMR consignment note.

---

[29] The CMR Convention is an instrument of international private law adopted in 1956. It governs the contractual relations for the international carriage of goods by road between the sender, the carrier, and the consignee. Kazakhstan and Uzbekistan acceded to the convention in 1995. Tajikistan did so in 1996.

[30] The 2008 protocol to the CRM Convention entered into force in 2011.

Railway Transport

Railway transport accounts for most of the international shipments between the STKEC region and the rest of the world and the transit shipments through the STKEC region. In 2018, two-thirds of the total value of the merchandise exports and imports of Sugd oblast was transported along the Bekabad–Nau railway, which connects Sugd oblast with Tashkent oblast. This railway was a conduit for almost all of Sugd oblasts' merchandise trade with Kazakhstan (Figure 7). Available data from indirect statistics suggest that railway transport accounts for four-fifths of cross-border cargo traffic in the Uzbek part of the STKEC region. In the Kazakh part of STKEC, most transit shipments are via railway transport, including shipments to and from the Uzbek and Tajik parts of the STKEC region.

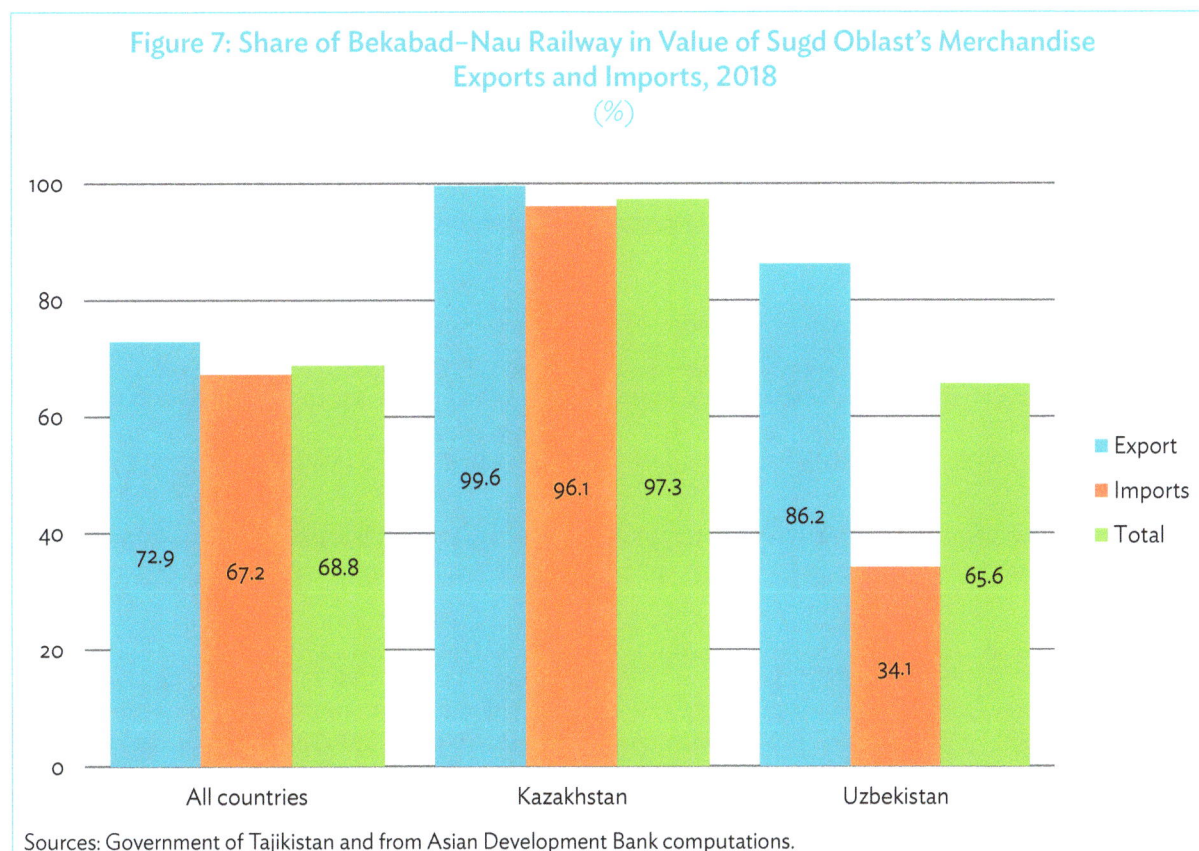

Figure 7: Share of Bekabad–Nau Railway in Value of Sugd Oblast's Merchandise Exports and Imports, 2018 (%)

Sources: Government of Tajikistan and from Asian Development Bank computations.

Railway infrastructure. There are major weaknesses and gaps in the railway infrastructure of the STKEC region. The railway network was mostly built during the former Soviet Union period and cannot meet the region's current and future needs. Many sections of the Turkestan–Shymkent railway are in poor condition, which increases considerably the transport time between these two cities. Most railway shipments to Uzbekistan pass through one of the two rail yards (sorting stations) located in Tashkent city. The capacity of these rail yards is not sufficient to accommodate so much traffic, causing significant delays in rail shipments to Uzbekistan, including the Uzbek part of the STKEC region. In the Tajik part of the region, there is no railway link between the southern part of Sugd oblast (where the Nau railway station is situated) and the northern part of the oblast where the Sugd free economic zone (FEZ) is located and major mining companies operate.[31] This increases the cost of freight shipments between the two oblasts and hinders their industrial development.

---

[31]   The Sirdarya River separates the two parts of the oblast.

Kazakhstan is undertaking a feasibility study of a high-speed railway from Turkestan city to Tashkent city via Shymkent. If this study finds the railway to be economically and financially viable and the railway is built, it will improve transport connectivity not only within the Kazakh part of the STKEC region, but also between its Kazakh and Uzbek parts. It will reduce the average travel time by rail between Turkestan and Tashkent via Shymkent—from 6.5–7.0 hours to 2.5 hours. Afterward, the railway could be extended to Khujand. The railway, once constructed, will provide a major boost to the tourism industry in the STKEC region.

Rolling stock. STKEC countries need to modernize their rolling stock to improve the efficiency and quality of railway services in the region. Uzbekistan also needs to increase its fleet of freight wagons to reduce the cost of cargo shipments by rail. The shortage of freight wagons often causes delays in the return of other countries' wagons from Uzbekistan. This increases the cost of cargo shipments to Uzbekistan because owners of wagons from other countries (e.g., Kazakhstan) have become reluctant to lease out their wagons for shipments to Uzbekistan. They charge a higher fee for shipments to Uzbekistan and goods transported to Uzbekistan are often transshipped from rail to road transport in Turkestan oblast. This increases cross-border road traffic between Kazakhstan and Uzbekistan and contributes to delays at the road BCPs between the two countries. Uzbekistan can quickly eliminate the shortage of freight wagons by allowing private companies to own and lease out such wagons, as Kazakhstan did in the 2000s.

Railway tariffs. Tariffs that the Kazakhstan Railways charges for transit cargo shipments are considerably higher than the tariffs for shipments to, from, or within Kazakhstan. This is one reason why goods transported to Uzbekistan are transshipped from rail to road transport in Turkestan oblast. When goods are to be transported from third countries (e.g., the PRC and the Russian Federation) to Uzbekistan via Kazakhstan, it is often cheaper to transport them to Turkestan oblast by rail, transfer them to trucks there, and then transport them to Uzbekistan by road.

Uzbekistan Railways also charge higher tariffs for transit shipments than for domestic, export, or import shipments. However, Uzbekistan Railways often gives discounts on transit shipments to or from Tajikistan, which accounts for most of transit shipments by rail in Uzbekistan.

Information and communication technologies. STKEC countries can considerably improve the efficiency and quality of railway transport services by introducing modern information and communication technologies (ICTs) in railway transport. By collaborating in the introduction of such technologies, STKEC countries can increase their benefits. For instance, the benefits of radio frequency identification (RFID) technology will be greater if two or all of the STKEC countries introduce it and make their systems interoperable.

Planned or proposed actions. To improve railway transport connectivity in the STKEC region, the following actions are planned or proposed:

(i)   Build a new railway yard in Tashkent oblast, near the border with Turkestan oblast.

(ii)   Upgrade existing railway infrastructure through track strengthening, electrification, and installation of modern signalling systems.

(iii) Complete the feasibility study of a Turkestan–Shymkent–Tashkent high-speed railway.

(iv)   Conduct a feasibility study of a railway link between the southern and the northern parts of Sugd oblast.

(v)   Construct these railways if the feasibility studies find them to be economically and financially viable.

(vi)   Increase the fleet of freight wagons in Uzbekistan through greater private sector involvement in railway transport operations.

(vii) Reduce the differences between the railway tariffs for transit and domestic, export, and import freight shipments.

(viii) Introduce modern ICTs in railway transport, such as RFID technology, through regional collaboration.

4.2 Modernization of Border Crossing Points and Border Management

The high cost—in terms of money and time—of crossing borders inside the STKEC region is a major impediment to the economic integration of the Kazakh, Uzbek, and Tajik parts of the region. To overcome this impediment and considerably reduce the cost and time, it will be imperative to develop the STKEC region—which in turn requires the modernization of BCPs and border management. Critical to such development is modernizing the road and railway BCPs given their pivotal role in the economic activities in the region.

Road and railway BCPs. There are eight road and railway BCPs inside the STKEC region (henceforth referred to as the STKEC BCPs). Five of these are located at the border between Turkestan and Tashkent oblasts; the other three are situated at the border between Tashkent and Sugd oblasts.[32] Most of the STKEC BCPs are located along one or two CAREC transport corridors (Tables 6 and 7).

Table 6: Border Crossing Points between Turkestan and Tashkent Oblasts

Name of Kazakh Side of BCP	Name of Uzbek Side of BCP	Mode of Transport	CAREC Corridors
Zhibek Zholy	Gisht Kuprik	Road (passenger traffic only)	3 and 6
Konysbayev	Yallama	Road	3 and 6
Kaplanbek	Navoi	Road	None
Kazygurt	Najimov	Road	None
Saryagash	Keles	Railway	3 and 6

BCP = border crossing point, CAREC = Central Asia Regional Economic Cooperation.

Source: Information provided by various stakeholders during interviews.

Table 7: Border Crossing Points between Tashkent and Sugd Oblasts

Name of Uzbek Side of BCP	Name of Tajik Side of BCP	Mode of Transport	CAREC Corridor
Oybek	Fotehobod	Road	2
Bekabad avto	Khashtyak	Road	None
Bekabad	Nau	Railway	2

BCP = border crossing point, CAREC = Central Asia Regional Economic Cooperation.

Source: Information provided by various stakeholders during interviews.

---

[32] There are four more BCPs between Turkestan oblast and Uzbekistan and nine more BCPs between Sugd oblast and Uzbekistan. There are also BCPs between Sugd oblast and the Kyrgyz Republic; and at the airports in Shymkent, Tashkent, and Khujand cities.

Fully functioning and efficient STKEC BCPs are indispensable in the economic activities of the region. All trade flows among the Kazakh, Uzbek, and Tajik parts of the region go through these BCPs, as well as large proportions of trade flows between the STKEC region and the rest of the world. Most of the transit trade flows also pass through STKEC BCPs. In addition, millions of people pass through the STKEC BCPs every year, with about 25,000 persons passing through the Zhibek Zholy–Gisht Kuprik BCP per day on average. The BCPs between Tashkent and Sugd oblasts are important not only for Sugd oblast, but also for the entire Tajikistan (Box 1).

Box 1: Importance of the Border Crossing Points between Sugd and Tashkent Oblasts for Tajikistan

The border crossing points (BCPs) between Sugd and Tashkent oblasts are important gateways for the movement of goods and people to and from Tajikistan. In 2018, around one-fifth of Tajikistan's total merchandise trade—including the bulk of its trade with Uzbekistan and over a half of its trade with Kazakhstan—passed through these BCPs (Table B.1).

Table B.1: Tajikistan: Exports, Imports, and Transit Trade through Border Crossing Points between Sugd and Tashkent Oblasts, 2018
($ million)

Name of Tajik Side of BCP	Exports			Imports			Transit	
	All countries	Kazakhstan	Uzbekistan	All countries	Kazakhstan	Uzbekistan	Incoming	Outgoing
Fotehobod	102.6	0.9	4.1	144.1	4.0	11.9	39.5	7.2
Khashtyak	0.2	0.0	0.2	1.3	0.0	1.3	0.0	0.0
Nau	424.9	297.8	86.6	1,017.8	506.0	22.4	1.1	1.5
Total	**527.6**	**298.7**	**90.9**	**1,163.3**	**510.0**	**35.6**	**40.6**	**8.7**

BCP = border crossing point.

Source: Government of Tajikistan.

Some 0.6 million people, including 0.4 million citizens of Tajikistan, entered the country through these BCPs. Of the 0.2 million foreigners who entered Tajikistan through these BCPs (comprising 19.7% of foreigners who visited the country in 2018), more than half were citizens of Uzbekistan (Table B.2).

Table B.2: Movement of People through Border Crossing Points between Sugd and Tashkent Oblasts, 2018
('000)

Name of Tajik Side of BCP	To Tajikistan			From Tajikistan		
		of which:			of which:	
	All persons	Citizens of Tajikistan	Citizens of Uzbekistan	All persons	Citizens of Tajikistan	Citizens of Uzbekistan
Fotehobod	451,072	297,610	70,178	452,033	299,729	68,873
Khashtyak	99,946	51,034	48,912	108,662	61,420	47,242
Nau	18,739	16,802	0	22,968	20,650	14
Total	**569,757**	**365,446**	**119,090[a]**	**583,663**	**381,799[b]**	**116,129**

BCP = border crossing point.

[a]   16.2% of the citizens of Uzbekistan visited Tajikistan in 2018.

[b]   21.5% of the citizens of Tajikistan visited Uzbekistan in 2018.

Source: Government of Tajikistan.

continued on next page

Box 1 *continued*

The movement of goods, vehicles, and people through the road BCPs between the Sugd and Tashkent oblasts increased considerably during the past several years. The total value of Tajikistan's merchandise exports passing through these BCPs rose almost fivefold between 2016 and 2019. The number of road vehicles passing through these BCPs increased more than 5 times, while the number of people increased 50 times over the same period (Table B.3).

Table B.3: Tajikistan: Movement of Goods, Vehicles, and People through Road Border Crossing Points between Sugd and Tashkent Oblasts, 2006–2009

	2016	2017	2018	2019
Movement of goods ($ million)				
Exports	18.6	27.1	102.8	86.3
Imports	91.6	103.2	145.4	169.4
Transit				
Incoming	31.6	22.8	39.5	10.1
Outgoing	11.5	20.9	7.2	2.4
Movement of road vehicles ('000)				
Arrivals	6.9	9.8	21.2	37.0
Departures	5.4	7.6	16.8	30.7
Movement of people ('000)				
Arrivals	13.1	17.8	551.0	677.5
Departures	13.0	17.3	560.7	699.2

Source: Government of Tajikistan.

Cost of border crossing. As the cross-border movement of goods, vehicles, and people increased during the past several years, crossing borders through STKEC BCPs also became costly—in terms of time needed and unofficial payments made. Vehicles often spend many hours just to pass through STKEC BCPs. Data from the CAREC Corridor Performance Measurement and Monitoring revealed that in 2019, trucks from Uzbekistan going to Kazakhstan took an average of 21.5 hours to clear through the Yallama–Konysbayev BCP. Trucks from Uzbekistan going to Tajikistan needed 3.1 hours on average to pass through the Oybek–Fotehobod BCP. Freight trains from Kazakhstan going to Uzbekistan took an average of 12 hours to clear through the Saryagash–Keles BCP.[33] Drivers often make unofficial payments to expedite the clearance of goods and vehicles through STKEC BCPs.

The high cost of border crossing for goods and trucks increases trade costs, making goods produced in the STKEC region less competitive in foreign markets, domestic prices of imported goods higher, and transit trade less cost-efficient. These are particularly detrimental to trade in perishable goods, such as fresh fruits and vegetables. Delays and other inconveniences that people experience when crossing STKEC BCPs also impede the development of regional tourism.

Border crossing point infrastructure and equipment. The high cost of border crossing in the STKEC region are partly due to inadequate infrastructure and lack of modern equipment at the BCPs. At most road BCPs, lanes for vehicles are insufficient to handle the volume of traffic. No separate lanes are allotted for trucks transporting

---

[33] By comparison, in 2019, it took trucks less than 2 hours on average to pass through the Dustlik–Dostuk BCP between Uzbekistan and the Kyrgyz Republic in either direction. Freight trains from Afghanistan going to Turkmenistan just take an average of 7.6 hours to clear through the Torghondi–Serkhet Abad BCP.

perishable goods. Instead, passenger and freight vehicles are funneled into the same lanes, thus, the processing of passenger and freight traffic is not streamlined. Customs information systems often malfunction, causing delays in the processing of freight traffic. Nonintrusive inspection equipment, such as x-ray machines, are either unavailable or old and often inoperable. Partly due to this situation, customs officers rely on manual inspections of vehicles and cargo, which takes more time. Vehicle scales are not automated and have low accuracy, which allows for too much discretion among scale operators. Since the equipment needed to inspect luggage inside passenger vehicles is not available, people who cross borders in vehicles need to take out their luggage and go through the luggage control for pedestrians. The layout of BCPs also requires people to carry their luggage over long distances in the open air to pass through the BCPs.

The governments of STKEC countries recognize the need to modernize BCPs on their common borders in a coordinated fashion. In 2017, Kazakhstan and Uzbekistan agreed on a road map to renovate and modernize the BCPs along their common border. From 2018 to 2019, they renovated, expanded, and modernized the facilities for processing pedestrian traffic at the Zhibek Zholy–Gisht Kuprik BCP. They are currently building new facilities for processing passenger vehicles at this BCP. Crossing the border through the Zhibek Zholy–Gisht Kuprik BCP has become much easier for pedestrians. It will also become easier for people who cross the border in vehicles once the new facilities for processing passenger vehicles are completed. The throughput capacity of the BCP will double from 25,000 to 50,000 persons per day.

In 2019, Kazakhstan and Uzbekistan began renovating and modernizing the Konysbayev–Yallama BCP. They are also building truck terminals near this BCP. The number of lanes for vehicles will be increased—from one to three for each direction of traffic—and new vehicle scanning and weighing equipment will be installed at the BCP. The truck terminals will have facilities for customs clearance of exports and imports.

Tajikistan and Uzbekistan have also agreed to modernize the BCPs along their common border, including the border between Sugd and Tashkent oblasts. However, this modernization has yet to begin due to lack of financing.

Border management. Another reason for the high cost of border crossing is the weakness in border management. In all three STKEC countries, there are several border agencies that execute border control and these lack coordination and cooperation. With a few exceptions, each type of border control is performed by a separate agency (Table 8). Single Window facilities are not yet installed at STKEC BCPs, however, Kazakhstan already launched a Single Window portal for foreign trade in April 2019 and Tajikistan began piloting an electronic Single Window for foreign trade in November 2019.[34] The border agencies usually carry out border controls consecutively. A hard copy of the same document often has to be submitted to several border agencies.

Data exchange among most of the border agencies is inadequate. Many "on-the-border" offices of agencies demand hard copies of documents issued by "behind-the-border" offices of the same agencies. Typographical errors or other mistakes in paper documents committed by staff of a "behind-the-border" office sometimes cause considerable delays just to secure a clearance for exports from an "on-the-border" office of the same agency.

Border agencies of STKEC countries also lack collaboration. There are no joint border controls at STKEC BCPs. In 2018, the customs agencies of Kazakhstan and Uzbekistan signed an agreement on mutual recognition of customs control of certain types of goods. However, this agreement only covers a small number of goods. There are no such agreements between the customs agencies of Kazakhstan and Tajikistan nor between Tajikistan and Uzbekistan.

---

[34]   Uzbekistan plans to launch an electronic Single Window for foreign trade by the end of 2020.

Table 8: Border Agencies in STKEC Countries

Agency	Types of Border Control Undertaken
Kazakhstan	
Border Service of the National Security Committee	Border crossing, documents, and visa control
State Revenue Committee of the Ministry of Finance (Subcommittee on Customs Control)	Customs control, and customs declaration and clearance for goods and vehicles
Committee of Veterinary Control and Supervision of the Ministry of Agriculture	State sanitary and veterinary control, inspection and verification of animal origin products, and issuance of veterinary certificates (permits) for regulated products
Committee of State Inspection in the Agricultural Sector of the Ministry of Agriculture	State phytosanitary and quarantine control, inspection and verification of plant origin products, and issuance of phytosanitary and quarantine certificates (permits) for regulated products
Tajikistan	
State Border Service of State National Security Committee	Border crossing and visa regime control
State Customs Service	Customs clearance procedures for goods and vehicles
State Committee of Food Safety	Plant quarantine and animal products inspection and verification
Sanitary and Epidemiological Service under the Ministry of Health[a]	Sanitary and epidemiological control for potential diseases
Uzbekistan	
State Border Service	Border crossing and visa regime
State Customs Committee	Single Window and customs clearance
State Inspection on Plant Quarantine	Inspection of plant origin products and issuance of import permit
State Veterinary Committee	Inspection of animal origin products and issuance of sanitary veterinary expertise and/or conclusion
Agency on Sanitary and Epidemiological Wellbeing	Sanitary-epidemiological control at the border

STKEC = Shymkent-Tashkent-Khujand Economic Corridor.

[a] Work is underway to make the Sanitary and Epidemiological Service independent from the Ministry of Health.

Sources: Relevant laws and codes of the three countries and consultations with relevant state agencies.

Most goods passing through STKEC BCPs undergo one or more physical inspections when they are not transported in a sealed compartment, container, or wagon. Although the customs agencies of Kazakhstan and Uzbekistan have adopted a risk management system, Kazakh and Uzbek customs officials at STKEC BCPs still physically inspect most incoming shipments. The customs agency of Tajikistan has not yet adopted a risk management system, and its officials at the STKEC BCPs physically inspect all incoming shipments. None of the border agencies in charge of phytosanitary and veterinary controls in all STKEC countries have adopted risk management systems. Hence, at STKEC BCPs, their officials physically inspect all incoming shipments that are subject to phytosanitary or veterinary controls.

Kazakh customs officials at the Saryagash–Keles BCP often physically inspect goods transported by rail via Kazakhstan to Uzbekistan, even when these goods are transported in a sealed container or a wagon. For this purpose, the container or wagon is usually taken to a privately owned rail yard where its cargo is unloaded, inspected, and then reloaded. The process increases not only the transit time, but also the transport cost because the freight forwarder pays for the unloading, reloading, and other services provided by the rail yard. In addition, the practice of using the services of a private rail yard to undertake customs inspections of goods creates opportunities for corruption.

All vehicles passing through STKEC BCPs undergo a physical inspection on both sides of the BCPs. Inspections done on inbound vehicles on the Uzbek side of the BCPs between Tashkent and Sugd oblasts are often quite intrusive and time-consuming. When passing through road STKEC BCPs, trucks are weighed on both sides of the BCPs.

People passing through the STKEC BCPs experience delays and other inconveniences not only because of poor infrastructure but also due to cumbersome border-crossing procedures. No green lanes are allotted for people—even if the infrastructure permits having such lanes (e.g., the Zhibek Zholy–Gisht Kuprik BCP). STKEC countries perform passport control of pedestrians twice on each side of the road BCPs.

Thus, to significantly reduce the cost of border crossing, STKEC countries need to modernize not only BCP infrastructure and equipment but also border crossing procedures. They need to establish electronic Single Window facilities at STKEC BCPs and to transition from heavy reliance on physical inspections to risk management. They can further facilitate trade in the region by harmonizing their data requirements for customs clearance of goods, and by establishing cross-border electronic exchange of data among their Single Windows for foreign trade. All these will reduce the cost of border crossing for people, goods, and vehicles. To reduce the budgetary expenditure on border management, they also need to set up joint customs, transport, and SPS controls at STKEC BCPs, which is similar to the joint customs control at BCPs between the PRC and Mongolia (Box 2).

Box 2: Joint Customs Control at Border Crossing Points between the People's Republic of China and Mongolia

In September 1993, the People's Republic of China (PRC) and Mongolia signed an Agreement on Customs Mutual Assistance and Cooperation to promote good relations, facilitate the flow of goods and passengers, and cooperate in preventing customs offenses. This was the legal basis for piloting a joint customs control (JCC) to address serious delays at the Erenhot/Erlian (PRC)–Zamyn-Uud (Mongolia) and Gantsmod/Ganqimaodao (PRC)–Gashuunsukhait (Mongolia) border crossing points (BCPs). A steering group comprising high-level officials from the Mongolia Customs General Administration (MCGA) and the General Administration of China Customs (GACC), together with technical working groups composed of field office personnel, were established at the BCP level.

The first phase of document harmonization was through a unified cargo manifest (UCM), which standardized essential cargo information, taking 25 data elements from the MCGA Customs declaration and GACC cargo manifest. The UCM was introduced at the Erenhot/Erlian–Zamyn-Uud BCP in 2009 and at the Gantsmod/Ganqimaodao–Gashuunsukhait BCP in 2011, and all trucks were required to use it. A PRC–Mongolia JCC Operation Process was written to guide the implementation and a specific printing system was employed to produce a unified format.

By introducing the UCM, the two BCPs eliminated the difficulties of translating and the repetitive filling out of forms. A feedback mechanism that verifies the entries ensured that the exchanged information were consistent, thereby cutting down processing time. MCGA reduced its procedures from 11 to 7 steps and as a result, the average waiting time for trucks dropped. Both the PRC and Mongolia customs administrations showed improved consistency in implementing customs control measures. The number of reported irregularities (e.g., false declarations, undervaluation, underweighting, and forged documents) decreased and compliance was strengthened.

The JCC initiative also paved the way for greater cooperation: GACC and MCGA established a regular meeting schedule to evaluate control operation data and communicate and solve problems as soon as possible. In 2010, the two countries signed a Protocol on Cooperation and Reciprocal Assistance in the Field of Customs, and in June 2017, also signed the Agreement to Improve Cooperation on Risk Management. Among their planned next steps are expanding the UCM to other BCPs, data sharing and paperless clearance, and mutual recognition of customs control or inspection result.

Source: ADB. 2019. *Modernization of Sanitary and Phytosanitary Measures in CAREC: An Assessment and the Way Forward.* Manila.

Customs transit. The expenses and delays in the customs transit of goods considerably increased trade costs in the STKEC region.[35] A large percentage of intraregional export and import shipments and most transit shipments by road in the region are made using the Transports Internationaux Routiers or International Road Transport (TIR) system.[36] Trucks that transport goods under a TIR carnet can pass through BCPs relatively faster because customs officials do not physically inspect their cargo. These trucks are not required to join a customs convoy. Nevertheless, using the TIR system increases trade costs for several reasons. Trucks that meet the TIR requirements are expensive, so road transport operators charge higher fees for such trucks. Second, TIR carnets cost several hundred US dollars. Third, the procedure for obtaining a TIR carnet is rather cumbersome and time-consuming. Hence, using the TIR system is only cost-effective when high-value goods are being transported by road across multiple borders.

When a truck is transporting goods without a TIR carnet, it is required to join a customs convoy (i.e., a group of trucks escorted by traffic police and a customs official) at the BCP of entry or at the inland customs clearance point. The truck driver must pay a fee for joining a customs convoy, increasing transport cost. Customs convoys depart from STKEC BCPs only a few times a day, so trucks often wait for hours to join one of these convoys, considerably increasing transport time.

STKEC countries can facilitate customs transit by introducing the electronic TIR (eTIR) system, Admission Temporaire/Temporary Admission (ATA) carnet system, and CAREC Advanced Transit System/Information Common Exchange (CATS/ICE).[37] Introducing the eTIR system would expedite the issuance of TIR carnets and enable customs agencies to conduct risk assessments prior to the arrival of cargo at BCPs. Implementing the ATA system would facilitate customs transit of goods when they are exported or imported temporarily. By introducing the CATS/ICE, traders would be able to obtain "comprehensive guarantees" covering multiple customs transit operations over a specified period of time. It would also lower the cost of guarantees for compliant traders.

STKEC countries can further facilitate transit trade by appointing national transit coordinators and local transit contacts. The national transit coordinators would coordinate the implementation of the eTIR system, ATA carnet system, and CATS/ICE and serve as national focal points on all matters concerning customs transit. The local transit contacts would collaborate with each other; and with the national transit coordinators, customs agencies, traders, and transport operators to ensure the correct application of transit procedures under various transit systems.

Planned and/or proposed actions. The following actions are planned or proposed to reduce the cost of border crossing in the STKEC region:

(i)   Complete the construction of a new passenger vehicle terminal at the Zhibek Zholy–Gisht Kuprik BCP.

(ii)   Complete the modernization of the Konysbayev–Yallama BCP.

(iii)   Modernize infrastructure and equipment at other STKEC BCPs.

(iv)   Separate passenger traffic from freight traffic at road BCPs.

---

[35]   Customs transit is a customs procedure where goods are transported, without paying import duties and taxes, between a BCP and an inland customs clearance point or between two or more BCPs.

[36]   The TIR system is a multilateral customs transit system based on the Customs Convention on the International Transport of Goods under Cover of TIR Carnets (TIR Convention). All three STKEC countries are Contracting Parties of the TIR Convention.

[37]   The eTIR system is the TIR system with electronic exchange of information among the carnet holders, customs agencies, and the TIR guarantee chain. The ATA carnet system is a multilateral system for tax- and duty-free temporary admission of goods into a customs territory. It is based on the Istanbul Convention. Of the three STKEC countries, only Kazakhstan accepts ATA carnets at present. The CATS/ICE is the electronic customs transit system that was developed under the CAREC program.

(v)   Establish electronic Single Window facilities at all STKEC BCPs.

(vi)   Harmonize data requirements for customs clearance of goods and establish an exchange of data system among the electronic Single Windows for foreign trade.

(vii) Transition from reliance on physical inspections to risk management.

(viii) Introduce the eTIR system, ATA carnet system, and CATS/ICE.

(ix)   Establish green lanes for trucks transporting perishable goods and/or using the TIR system, eTIR system, ATA carnet system, or CATS/ICE system.

(x)   Appoint a national transit coordinator in each STKEC country and local transit contacts to facilitate transit trade in the region.

(xi)   Conduct regular Time Release Studies covering the main STKEC BCPs.

(xii) Consider setting up joint customs, transport, and SPS controls at STKEC BCPs.

4.3   Development of Horticulture Value Chains

Agriculture is an important sector in the economy of Turkestan, Tashkent, and Sugd oblasts. It generates one-fifth of the gross regional product (GRP) of Turkestan and Sugd oblasts and one-third of the GRP of Tashkent oblast. Livelihoods of most people living in rural areas directly or indirectly depend on agriculture.[38] Cotton, fruits, vegetables, and livestock products comprise large proportions of total agricultural output in all three oblasts. Wheat accounts for a substantial share of agricultural output in Turkestan and Tashkent oblasts.

All three oblasts have considerable potential for expanding the production and export of fruits and vegetables. To realize this potential, they need to develop horticulture value chains. Since they face similar opportunities and challenges in increasing their production and export of fruits and vegetables, cross-border cooperation and integration in developing horticulture value chains can be very useful.

Horticulture value chains will make a major contribution to the development of the STKEC. It will boost economic activity and create many new jobs throughout the region. It will also foster technical progress and increase not only the gross value of exports, but also the share of value-added in exports.[39]

Opportunities in horticulture. The climatic conditions in the STKEC region are favorable for producing a wide variety of fruits and vegetables. Turkestan oblast is one of Kazakhstan's warmest provinces, while Tashkent oblast is one of Uzbekistan's most water-abundant provinces. In Sugd oblast, fruits ripen 10–20 days earlier than in other parts of Central Asia. Thanks in part to abundant sunshine, fruits and vegetables produced in this region have superior taste and nutritional qualities. Due to minimal use of chemicals in horticulture, the region has considerable potential for exports of organic produce.

Turkestan, Kazakhstan; Tashkent, Uzbekistan; and Sugd, Tajikistan are among the leading oblasts in the production of fruits and vegetables. Turkestan, for instance, accounts for 73% of grapes and 40% of other fruits produced in

---

[38]   In 2018, the rural population comprised four-fifths of the population of Turkestan oblast, half of the population of Tashkent oblast, and three-fourths of the population of Sugd oblast. Almost half of the population of the STKEC region (5.4 million people) lives in rural areas.

[39]   Horticulture is a labor-intensive agricultural activity. It becomes skill- and technology-intensive as it develops and undergoes modernization. Hence, horticulture product exports have more value added than many other exported crops, including cotton and wheat.

Kazakhstan.[40] Of the country's greenhouses, 80% are located in this oblast.[41] Almost half of Tajikistan's orchards, including more than four-fifths of its apricot orchards, are in Sugd oblast.[42]

The location of the STKEC region offers good opportunities for exporting horticulture products. Numerous countries that are net importers of fruits and vegetable cultivated in the STKEC region are situated close to (or at least not far away from) the region. These include the PRC, the Russian Federation, Germany, United Arab Emirates; and other Asian, European, and Middle Eastern countries. In 2018, the net imports of fruits and nuts amounted to $3.4 billion in the PRC and $5.0 billion in the Russian Federation (Table 9). Demand for many horticulture goods, including organic produce, is expected to grow rapidly in both the PRC and the Russian Federation over the medium term.[43]

Table 9: Net Imports of Selected Horticulture Products by the People's Republic of China, Germany, Russian Federation, and United Arab Emirates, 2018
($ million)

Horticulture Product	PRC	Russian Federation	Germany	UAE
Fresh grapes	(103.4)	322.2	676.9	42.1
Dried grapes	7.3	40.0	138.3	(0.7)
Fresh apricots	(0.9)	41.9	104.2	2.2
Other cherries	1,303.2	116.8	146.0	5.9
Plums and sloes	77.2	56.2	56.6	10.5
Dried apricots	5.0	19.1	19.3	1.8
Prunes	9.0	36.7	29.0	0.0
Walnuts, in shell	(50.0)	4.2	28.5	(17.5)
Walnuts, shelled	(65.9)	15.7	217.9	14.1
Total	**1,181.5**	**652.8**	**1,416.7**	**94.8**

PRC = People's Republic of China, UAE = United Arab Emirates, ( ) = negative.

Note: Net imports are equal to the difference between imports and exports.

Sources: United Nations Comtrade Database. https://comtrade.un.org/ (accessed 6 May 2020); and ADB estimates.

Actual output and exports of fruits and vegetables in the STKEC region are well below their potential levels. Fruits and vegetables account for a small percentage of merchandise exports of Turkestan, Tashkent, and Sugd oblasts. In 2018, edible vegetables and certain roots and tubers (horticulture goods included in Chapter 7 of the 2017 edition of the Harmonized System), and edible fruit and nuts and peels of citrus fruit or melons (Chapter 8) comprised 3.8% of merchandise exports of Turkestan oblast, 4.2% of merchandise exports of Tashkent oblast, and 3.0% of merchandise exports of Sugd oblast.[44]

---

[40]   Otyrar (Kazakhstan). https://otyrar.kz/2019/09/peredovye-tehnologii-v-apk-i-investitsionnyj-potentsial-regiona-itogi-razvitiya-turkestan skoj-oblasti-za-8-mesyatsev-2019-goda/.

[41]   Government of Kazakhstan. 2019. *Comprehensive Plan of Socio-Economic Development of Turkestan Oblast till 2024.* http://adilet.zan.kz/rus/docs/ P1800000938 [in Russian].

[42]   V. Leahu and N. Zevashoeva. 2015. *Apricot-Based Value Chains in Tajikistan: Dried Apricots and Apricots for Fresh Market.* Rome: Food and Agriculture Organization of the United Nations (FAO).

[43]   World Bank. 2019. *Central Asia's Horticulture Sector: Capitalizing on New Export Opportunities in Chinese and Russian Markets.* Washington, DC.

[44]   Shymkent and Tashkent cities also export horticulture products, but these are mostly produced in other parts of Kazakhstan and Uzbekistan. In 2018, horticulture products comprised 0.25% of the merchandise exports of Shymkent city and 3.7% for Tashkent city.

Weaknesses in horticulture value chains. Many factors hinder the production and exports of horticulture goods in the STKEC region. One of these is because the agriculture sector mostly consists of small commercial farms and noncommercial household farms.[45] There are only a few agricultural cooperatives and clusters and only a small proportion of the farms are members of an agricultural cooperative or part of an agricultural cluster.

Most small farms lack knowledge and financial resources to use modern agricultural technologies and best farming practices. They employ old agricultural technologies and poor farming practices. Hence, productivity in agriculture is low. The available data on crop yields in Kazakhstan, Tajikistan, and Uzbekistan indicate that the yield of major crops is significantly lower in the STKEC region, especially in its Kazakh and Tajik parts, than in countries such as Chile, the Netherlands, Turkey, and the United States (Table 10).

Table 10: Yield of Selected Crops in Kazakhstan, Tajikistan, Uzbekistan, and Comparator Countries, 2018
(ton/ha)

	Cotton	Wheat	Apples	Apricots	Grapes	Cherries	Potatoes	Tomatoes
STKEC Countries								
Kazakhstan	2.6	1.2	6.4	5.4	6.1	0.8	19.8	25.2
Tajikistan	1.6	3.0	5.6	3.0	7.3	n.a.	19.4	28.4
Uzbekistan	2.1	4.1	11.5	12.8	15.8	14.1	33.7	37.8
Comparator Countries								
Chile	n.a.	6.2	50.2	10.2	11.8	5.2	28.7	62.7
Netherlands	n.a.	8.8	40.8	n.a.	5.7	0.4	36.6	508.9
Turkey	5.0	2.7	20.8	6.0	9.4	7.6	33.5	68.9
United States	2.7	3.2	39.5	8.4	18.2	9.1	49.8	96.8

ha = hectare, n.a. = not applicable, STKEC = Shymkent–Tashkent–Khujand Economic Corridor.

Sources: Food and Agriculture Organization of the United Nations and Asian Development Bank estimates.

When the agriculture sector consists mostly of small farms, this constrains not only the production but also the export of horticulture goods. Exporting horticulture products requires (i) a good deal of information (such as SPS measures applied by both the exporting and importing countries), (ii) substantial human and financial resources to obtain various export certificates, (iii) making logistical arrangements for an international shipment, and (iv) financial resources to afford payment delays until after the importer receives the shipment, among many others. Most farms in the STKEC region do not have such information and resources so only a few of them are capable of exporting their produce by themselves. They usually sell their produce to local wholesale traders for cash immediately after harvest.

Major foreign buyers of horticulture products (e.g., modern supermarket and grocery store chains) usually require that products are supplied regularly in large quantities and with specific characteristics—in terms of safety, size, color, and others. They also require suppliers to be certified under certain food safety schemes recognized by the International Food Safety Initiative. For organic produce, modern retail chains require products to be certified under the International Federation of Organic Agriculture Movements (IFOAM) Family of Standards.

---

[45]   There are around 70,000 farms in Sugd oblast alone, according to the information provided by the Agriculture Department of the Sugd Oblast Administration.

Small farms cannot meet these requirements. Their production volumes are small and most of them could not adequately ensure the safety of the fruits and vegetables they produce. Very few of them are certified under standards included in the IFOAM Family of Standards and/or the Global G.A.P. scheme—the food safety scheme for fruits and vegetables recognized by the International Food Safety Initiative.

Even wholesale traders can rarely supply large quantities of fruits and vegetables with consistent quality. They purchase fruits and vegetables from several farms, which often have different characteristics. These traders also cannot guarantee a stable supply and the safety of their merchandise. Consequently, only a small portion of fruits and vegetables produced in the STKEC region are exported, with a tiny fraction of these exported as organic produce.

The Russian Federation's traditional food markets, which have less stringent requirements than modern food retail chains, account for most of the horticulture export goods from the STKEC region. Tashkent and Sugd oblasts also export their horticulture products to Kazakhstan, including Shymkent city and Turkestan oblast. Portions of Uzbek and Tajik horticulture goods imported to Kazakhstan are reexported to the Russian Federation as Kazakh products. This is to take advantage of the (i) lower railway tariffs for import and export shipments (compared with transit shipments) in Kazakhstan, and (ii) lower technical barriers to exports of Kazakh agricultural goods to the Russian Federation (because of Kazakhstan's membership in the Eurasian Economic Union [EAEU]).[46] As most of horticulture exports from the STKEC region directly or indirectly go to the Russian Federation, this makes these exports very sensitive to changes in the demand and regulations in their destination country.

Lack of water is another major factor that constrains the production of horticulture goods in the STKEC region, particularly in the Kazakh and Tajik parts. Most of the irrigation infrastructure are in poor condition, the use of water-saving agricultural technologies is limited, and the efficiency of water use is low in the region. The lack of water limits the land area from producing horticulture goods to its full potential. It also adversely impacts the yields of fruits and vegetables. In Sugd oblast, for instance, increasing the irrigated land area by 1 hectare can boost the annual output of potatoes by 40–50 tons.[47]

Agricultural research and development (R&D), agricultural extension services, and export promotion are weak. As a result, some of the crop varieties cultivated by the farmers are not suited to the region's climatic conditions. They have low yields and/or are vulnerable to pests that are widespread in the region. Due to underdeveloped agricultural extension services, most farmers are unfamiliar with modern agricultural technologies and best farming practices. As export promotion is weak, many farmers have little information about opportunities for exporting their produce and how they may avail of these.

Storage facilities and processing capacities are lacking, including primary processing capacities for horticulture products. Only a few modern cold storage facilities exist in Turkestan and Sugd oblasts. More of such facilities are found in Tashkent oblast and Tashkent city, but their total capacity is only enough to store and process a small fraction of the annual output of fruits and vegetables produced in Tashkent oblast.

As a result, postharvest losses in horticulture are considerable, the prices of fruits and vegetables fluctuate substantially throughout a year, and only a small percentage of horticulture output is processed. In Turkestan oblast, for instance, postharvest losses in horticulture reach 40% and only 2.5% of fruits and vegetables undergo processing.[48] In Uzbekistan, postharvest losses in horticulture reach 30% and only 15% of the total output of fruits

[46] Horticulture products are also exported from Tajikistan (particularly Sugd oblast) and from the eastern part of Uzbekistan to the Kyrgyz Republic (which is also an EAEU member)—for subsequent reexport to the Russian Federation.

[47] Information was provided by the Sugd oblast administration.

[48] Estimates were provided by representatives of the business community in Turkestan oblast.

and vegetables are processed.[49] In Sugd oblast, the share in the manufacturing of food products and beverages in gross industrial output decreased from 30.9% in 2014 to 21.2% in 2019.[50] The lack of primary processing (e.g., sorting and packaging) capacity not only also lowers export prices but also constrains exports as many foreign importers require that the fruits and vegetables be properly sorted and packaged.

Planned and/or proposed actions. To develop horticulture value chains in the STKEC region, the following actions are planned or proposed:

(i)   Rehabilitate and upgrade the irrigation infrastructure (e.g., in Asht and Match districts of Sugd oblast) and expand the use of water-saving technologies, such as drip irrigation.

(ii)   Promote the establishment of horticulture cooperatives and clusters by providing technical assistance to these cooperatives and clusters.

(iii)   Strengthen horticulture-related R&D by increasing government financing and ensuring greater private sector involvement to develop high-yield, early varieties of fruits and vegetables.

(iv)   Strengthen agricultural extension services to promote the introduction of new technologies and best farming practices in horticulture, such as precision agriculture and smart farming systems.

(v)   Promote cross-border collaboration in knowledge exchange, joint projects, and training programs in horticulture-related R&D, and in agricultural extension services.

(vi)   Develop horticulture support services, such as agronomy and plant protection services, and facilitate cross-border trade in these services.

(vii)   Establish a regional network of agro-logistics centers with modern cold-storage facilities and primary processing capacities.

(viii) Provide technical and financial support to horticulture cooperatives and clusters and agro-logistics centers in ensuring food safety, producing or supplying organic products, and obtaining international food quality certificates.

(ix)   Strengthen marketing and export promotion to support the export of horticulture products to new markets and market segments (e.g., the PRC, Germany, modern retail chains in the Russian Federation, online sale channels, and organic food retailers).

(x)   Promote cross-border collaboration among producers and exporters of fruits and vegetables that supply to modern retail chains in the Russian Federation, the PRC, and other countries.

(xi)   Develop and introduce digital applications that will provide farmers with up-to-date information on input and export markets for horticulture goods.

(xii)   Facilitate the establishment of regional online marketplaces for farm inputs and agricultural goods, including fruits and vegetables.

4.4   Modernization of Sanitary and Phytosanitary Measures and Development of Food Quality Certification Services

Like other countries, STKEC countries maintain sanitary and phytosanitary (SPS) measures to ensure food safety and prevent the spread of pests and diseases among animals and plants. In recent years, all three countries have

---

[49]   *Fergana.* 2019. Mirziyoyev Instructed to Reduce Losses During Harvesting and Make Money on Waste (in Russian). 7 May. https://fergana.agency/news/108745/.

[50]   The TA team's estimates are based on the data provided by the Government of Tajikistan.

made good progress in strengthening and modernizing their national SPS systems. However, weaknesses still exist. To reduce the incidence of food-borne diseases, raise productivity in agriculture, lower barriers to international trade in agricultural and food products, and boost exports of their products, they need to further strengthen their SPS systems. They also need to develop food quality certification services to gain access to new export markets and market segments for food products. Modernizing SPS measures and developing food quality certification services are essential to the development of STKEC because, as noted earlier, agriculture is a major sector of the economies of Turkestan, Tashkent, and Sugd oblasts and the region has considerable yet unrealized potential for increasing intraregional trade in food products and for exporting horticulture goods, including organic produce, to the rest of the world.

Membership in international organizations. Kazakhstan and Tajikistan are members of the World Trade Organization (WTO) and, as such, they are parties to the WTO Agreement on the Application of Sanitary and Phytosanitary Measures (the SPS Agreement), which sets out the rules for SPS measures maintained by WTO member countries (Box 3). Uzbekistan is an observer at the WTO. All three STKEC countries are members of the Codex Alimentarius Commission (Codex), which provides international standards, guidelines, and codes of practice relating to food safety. They are also members of the World Organisation for Animal Health (OIE), which sets international standards for animal health. They are Contracting Parties to the International Plant Protection Convention (IPPC), whose secretariat develops the International Standards for Phytosanitary Measures (ISPMs).

Box 3: The World Trade Organization Sanitary and Phytosanitary Measures Agreement

The World Trade Organization (WTO) Agreement on the Application of Sanitary and Phytosanitary Measures—or the SPS Agreement—sets out the basic rules of sanitary and phytosanitary (SPS) measures in WTO member countries. While recognizing the sovereign right of any government to protect human, animal, and plant life and health, the SPS Agreement aims to ensure that this sovereign right is not misused for protectionist purposes and do not result in unnecessary barriers to international trade. Accordingly, the agreement allows WTO member countries to maintain appropriate SPS protection but stipulates that SPS measures must be based on an analysis of scientific data and an assessment of the actual risks involved. They should be applied only to the extent necessary to protect human, animal, or plant life or health; and should not be used to arbitrarily or unjustifiably discriminate countries where identical or similar conditions prevail.

Though the SPS Agreement permits member countries to use different SPS standards and different methods of inspecting products, it also encourages member countries to harmonize their SPS measures—that is, to make them consistent with the international standards, guidelines, and recommendations developed by the following organizations:

- Codex Alimentarius Commission (Codex) for food safety,

- World Organisation for Animal Health (OIE) for animal health, and

- International Plant Protection Convention (IPPC) based on the Food and Agriculture Organization of the United Nations (FAO) for plant health.

Even if WTO member countries use different SPS standards, the SPS measures they apply should be accepted as equivalent if it can be shown that these measures provide the same level of health protection. Furthermore, member countries should recognize pest- and disease-free areas, which may not correspond to political boundaries. They should adapt their SPS requirements so that they are appropriate for products from these areas.

Source: World Trade Organization.

Sanitary and phytosanitary laws, standards, and regulations. All STKEC countries have laws on food safety, plant health, and animal health. The SPS standards they apply consist of regional and international standards—such as Government Standards and International Organization for Standardization standards—and nationally developed standards.[51] In Kazakhstan, the EAEU's SPS technical regulations apply, whereas Tajikistan and Uzbekistan both adhere to national SPS technical regulations.

The SPS legislation, standards, and regulations in STKEC countries and the technical regulations of EAEU's SPS are not fully harmonized with the standards, guidelines, and recommendations developed by the Codex, OIE, and IPPC Secretariat. Kazakhstan's legislation on animal health provides for the adoption of most, but not for all, of the key provisions of the Terrestrial Health Code of the OIE (or the OIE Code). Kazakhstan's Law on Safety of Foodstuffs provides for risk assessment but makes no reference to the Hazard Analysis and Critical Control Point (HACCP).[52] The country's Law on Plant Quarantine does not provide for the implementation of key ISPMs. In Tajikistan, the Law on Quality and Safety of Food provides for risk assessment and makes HACCP mandatory. The Law on Plant Quarantine is broadly in line with the IPPC. However, the Law on Veterinary makes limited provision for risk assessment. In Uzbekistan, the Law on Safety and Quality of Foodstuffs does not provide for risk assessment and makes no reference to HACCP. The Law on Veterinary provides for the adoption of only some of the key provisions of the OIE Code. The legislation on plant health does not provide for the implementation of the ISPMs. None of the STKEC countries have food safety parameters, such as maximum residue levels, that are fully aligned with the Codex standards. In Kazakhstan, the list of food safety parameters include quality parameters such as total count, mold, and yeast.[53] There are significant differences in SPS standards and regulations among STKEC countries, creating difficulties in the trade of agricultural and food products in the region.

Food safety systems. None of the STKEC countries have adopted the farm-to-fork approach to food safety. They rely more on inspection and certification of end products than on risk-based, process-focused food safety systems. Only a small percentage of businesses involved in the production and supply of food products in the STKEC region have adopted HACCP and/or its prerequisite programs, such as Good Agricultural Practices (GAP) and Good Hygiene Practices (GHP). Similarly, only a small number of businesses in the STKEC region have been certified under the food safety standards of the Global Food Safety Initiative (GFSI) or the ISO 22000—Food Safety Management Systems. Food traceability is inadequate in all STKEC countries.

There is no risk-based classification of imports of food products. A certificate of conformity and a sanitary import permit are required for all imports of food products and food safety test results are required before a certificate of conformity and a sanitary import permit can be issued.[54] Neither certificates of conformity nor sanitary import permits are issued electronically.

Animal health protection. STKEC countries, especially Kazakhstan and Uzbekistan, have been fairly effective in protecting animal health in recent years. No cases of the foot-and-mouth disease, sheep pox, and goat-pox have been recorded in STKEC countries for many years.[55] In 2017, the OIE recognized the entire Kazakhstan, including the Kazakh part of the STKEC region, as a free zone for foot-and-mouth disease.[56]

---

[51] GOSTs are regional standards maintained by the Euro-Asian Council for Standardization, Metrology, and Certification—a standards-setting organization operating under the auspices of the CIS. The ISO standards are the standards developed by the International Organization for Standardization (usually referred to as ISO).

[52] HACCP is a systematic approach to the identification, evaluation, and control of food safety hazards. The Codex recommends that HACCP be adopted wherever possible to enhance food safety.

[53] ADB. 2019. *Modernization of Sanitary and Phytosanitary Measures in CAREC: An Assessment and the Way Forward.* Manila.

[54] In addition, a veterinary or a phytosanitary import permit is required for imports of most food products.

[55] ADB. 2019. *Prevention and Control of Transboundary Animal Diseases in the CAREC Region. Concept Note.* Manila.

[56] *The Astana Times.* 2017. Kazakhstan Declared Foot-and-Mouth-Disease Free, Designation to Boost Exports. 30 May. https://astanatimes.com/2017/05/kazakhstan-declared-foot-and-mouth-disease-free-designation-to-boost-exports/.

Nonetheless, several transboundary animal diseases, such as brucellosis and rabies, are present in at least some of the STKEC countries. To prevent the spread of these diseases, enhance food safety, and facilitate trade in livestock and livestock products, STKEC countries need to further strengthen and modernize their animal health protection systems. They also need to strengthen their animal identification and traceability systems and modernize veterinary control over exports and imports. Staff training at the veterinary agencies of Tajikistan and Uzbekistan are needed, especially at their local branches in the STKEC region.

Veterinary control over international trade is arguably excessive in all STKEC countries. In Uzbekistan, for instance, two documents are required for all exports that are subject to veterinary control: a veterinary export permit and a veterinary certificate. A veterinary import permit is required for all imports of live animals and products of animal origin. There are six types of veterinary certificates for exports and three types of veterinary import permits. It takes up to 30 days to obtain a veterinary certificate for exports. A veterinary certificate (import permit) is also required for all exports (imports) of live animals and products of animal origin in Kazakhstan and Tajikistan. None of the STKEC countries have introduced electronic veterinary certificates and veterinary import permits or risk-based veterinary control over international trade.[57] Almost all imports of live animals and products of animal origin undergo physical veterinary inspection. However, Tajikistan's and Uzbekistan's veterinary services have limited capacity to detect animal diseases at BCPs due to lack of diagnostic equipment and quarantine facilities.

Plant protection. Effective and efficient plant protection requires pest surveillance and pest risk analysis. Pest surveillance generates data needed for the compilation of pest lists, pest risk analysis, pest reporting to other countries, phytosanitary certification of exports, and in establishing and maintaining pest-free areas.[58] It helps countries gain and maintain access to export markets for goods that are subject to phytosanitary measures. Pest risk analysis provides the rationale for phytosanitary measures, including phytosanitary import requirements. It helps protect plant health and life effectively without creating unnecessary barriers to imports.[59]

Unfortunately, STKEC countries do not conduct proper pest surveillance and pest risk analysis. The reasons include lack of financing and insufficient capacity of government agencies in charge of plant protection. They do maintain lists of quarantine pests, but these lists are not based on up-to-date surveillance data. When applying phytosanitary measures to imports, Kazakhstan uses the pest lists of the EAEU. These lists put emphasis on easily identifiable pests but not on bacteria, viruses, and some fungi that require sophisticated laboratory technology to identify them (footnote 53).

Given the proximity among the STKEC countries, pests such as locusts sometimes spread from one country to another. To prevent the spread of pests across their borders, STKEC countries signed bilateral agreements on collaboration in plant protection. However, these agreements are not fully implemented, and cross-border cooperation is lacking among the plant protection agencies of STKEC countries.

Phytosanitary control over exports and imports among STKEC countries constitutes a major barrier to trade, including trade in the STKEC region. A phytosanitary certificate is required for the export of plants and plant products and the procedures for obtaining it are cumbersome. Exporters need to obtain it even when the importing country does not require it. Since STKEC countries do not maintain up-to-date pest lists and have weak diagnostic capacity, the pest information included in phytosanitary certificates is often inaccurate. None of the STKEC countries have introduced an electronic phytosanitary certificate. Since phytosanitary control over imports is not yet based on risk management, all imports of plants and plant products are subject to physical

---

[57] Uzbekistan has only introduced a risk-based classification of products of animal origin for the issuance of veterinary certificates for exports.

[58] FAO. 2018. *ISPM 6–Surveillance*. Rome.

[59] FAO. 2016. *ISPM 2–Framework for Pest Risk Analysis*. Rome.

inspection, which can be time-consuming and creates opportunities for corruption. Inspectors at BCPs lack training, guidelines, and the equipment necessary for an effective phytosanitary control over imports. There are also no plant quarantine facilities at BCPs. Consequently, plants and plant products, such as cuttings and seeds, are often imported with pests.

Laboratory capacity. There are several dozens of SPS laboratories in the STKEC region, but many of them lack modern equipment and do not use modern testing methods. Different laboratories are able to conduct different types of chemical analyses, but no laboratory is able to analyze the entire series of chemical contaminants as required in the Codex General Standard for Contaminants and Toxins in Food and Feed. Food microbiology laboratories use the classic methods—which take 3–4 days to produce results—to analyze pathogenic bacteria. They are unable to analyze emerging pathogenic bacteria, such as strains of salmonella. Most food safety laboratories do not apply the Codex standards for sampling procedures, such as the General Guidelines on Sampling and the Principles for the Use of Sampling and Testing in International Food Trade. None of the veterinary laboratories, including Uzbekistan's central veterinary laboratory in Tashkent, are able to perform all OIE-listed tests.[60] Phytosanitary laboratories lack the diagnostic capacity to detect and identify fungi, bacteria, phytoplasmas, and viruses that cannot be reliably diagnosed by culturing and/or microscopy (footnote 53).

None of the SPS laboratories in the STKEC region are internationally accredited to ISO 17025:2017.[61] Foreign regulatory bodies generally do not accept test results from these laboratories. This creates an additional difficulty in exporting agricultural and food products from the STKEC region. When these products are exported to countries with stringent SPS requirements (e.g., European Union [EU] countries), they usually undergo tests at foreign laboratories at considerable cost to the exporters. Hence, exports of agricultural and food products from the STKEC region mostly go to countries with relatively loose SPS requirements or to those that accept test results from laboratories without ISO 17025 international accreditation (e.g., the Russian Federation).

To boost such exports (especially to nontraditional export markets and market segments such as Germany, the PRC, the United Arab Emirates, and the Russian Federation retail chains), the STKEC region needs SPS laboratories that are internationally accredited to ISO 17025:2017. Such accreditation should cover the important animal diseases, plant pests, and food safety parameters. Given their limited financial and human resources, it will be more cost-effective to set up right in the STKEC region a network of SPS laboratories that are internationally accredited to ISO 17025:2017 for different tests, and then provide testing services to businesses in all STKEC countries.

Food quality certification services. Food quality certification services are underdeveloped in STKEC countries, with no or weak competition in some segments of the market for these services. Only the national standards-setting bodies are allowed to issue certificates of conformity (based on national standards) for imported food products. A few firms—all or most of which are subsidiaries of foreign companies—can issue a certificate under a GFSI-recognized food safety scheme and/or a standard included in the IFOAM Family of Standards. These firms engage foreign experts to conduct audits, and their services are expensive. Similarly, a few firms can help food

---

[60]   Of the veterinary laboratories in STKEC countries, only Kazakhstan's National Veterinary Reference Center, which is based in Nur-Sultan, can perform all these tests.

[61]   The ISO/IEC 17025:2017—General Requirements for the Competence of Testing and Calibration Laboratories is the main ISO standard used by testing and calibration laboratories. It specifies the required competence, impartiality, and consistent operation of laboratories. A laboratory is considered to have ISO/IEC 17025:2017 international accreditation if it is accredited under this standard by a body that is a member of the International Laboratory Accreditation Cooperation (ILAC). Only Kazakhstan's National Accreditation Center is a member of the ILAC. Some SPS laboratories in the Kazakh part of the STKEC region and one SPS laboratory located in Khujand are accredited by Kazakhstan's National Accreditation Center. However, their accreditation is not based on ISO 170257:2017.

producers implement HACCP and its prerequisite programs and, if needed, obtain an ISO 22000 certificate. This partly explains why only a small number of food-producing companies in the STKEC region have an HACCP certificate, an ISO 22000 certificate, and/or a certificate under a GFSI-recognized food safety scheme. Without these certificates, many food producers in the STKEC region find it difficult to export their products. STKEC countries can improve the availability of food quality certification services if they offer regional training courses in HACCP, GAP, GHP, ISO 22000, selected GFSI-recognized food safety schemes, and organic food regulations in major export markets. They could also enhance competition in the market for certification services by liberalizing cross-border trade in these services.

Planned and/or proposed action. To modernize the SPS measures in the STKEC countries and develop food safety certification services in the STKEC region, the following actions are planned or proposed:

(i)   Establish regional training programs in international SPS standards and best practices for the staff of SPS agencies.

(ii)   Harmonize the SPS laws, standards, and regulations of the STKEC countries with the standards, guidelines, and recommendations developed by the Codex, OIE, and IPPC Secretariat.

(iii)   Make SPS certificates optional for exports so that exporters will not have to obtain an SPS certificate if it is not required in an importing country.

(iv)   Introduce electronic SPS certificates and permits (including electronic veterinary and phytosanitary certificates) and ensure mutual recognition of the electronic certificates by all three countries.

(v)   Transition to risk-based SPS control over international trade with risk-based categorization of imports subject to SPS measures.

(vi)   Establish plant and animal quarantine facilities at selected STKEC BCPs.

(vii)   Provide veterinary and phytosanitary inspectors at STKEC BCPs with equipment and guidelines needed to perform effective risk-based physical inspections.

(viii) Establish a network of SPS laboratories with ISO 17025:2017 international accreditation in the STKEC region.

(ix)   Start conducting pest surveillance, compiling pest lists, and carrying out pest risk analysis in accordance with relevant ISPMs.

(x)   Offer regional training courses in HACCP, GAP, GHP, ISO 22000, selected GFSI-recognized food safety schemes, and organic food regulations in major export markets for organic food products (e.g., the European Union).

(xi)   Enhance competition in the market for food quality certification services, such as by liberalizing cross-border trade in these services.

(xii)   Incentivize food producers to implement HACCP and its prerequisite programs; and to obtain an ISO 22000 certificate, a certificate under a GFSI-recognized food safety scheme, and a certificate under an organic food standard included in the IFOAM Family of Standards.

(xiii) Strengthen the food traceability systems and adopt the farm-to-fork approach to food safety.

(xiv)   Establish a regional animal identification and traceability system to prevent and control animal diseases and ensure that livestock and livestock products could be traced.

(xv)   Pursue closer cross-border collaboration (in the form of data exchange, joint training programs, and others) among SPS agencies and their local offices in the STKEC region.

4.5   Development of Regional Tourism

Shymkent and Tashkent cities; and also Turkestan, Tashkent, and Sugd oblasts have many tourism assets, including cultural heritage sites and natural landscapes. Cross-border cooperation in tourism development can help them boost intraregional tourism and increase the number of tourist arrivals from outside the region. By combining their tourism assets, they can attract more international tourists than when done individually. Collectively, they can offer more diversified and tailored tourism products that cater to the different tastes and demands of a broader market. Tourism destinations and experiences in the STKEC region can also be integrated with well-known ones outside the region, such as Samarkand and the Fergana Valley, to further increase their appeal. Tackling tourism development in an integrative way can also create more jobs and boost overall tourism revenue. Extensive cooperation and dynamic collaboration can be done in various aspects, such as tourism infrastructure and services, product development, quality standards, tourism skills, branding and marketing, statistics, and market intelligence.

International visitor arrivals in STKEC countries. While a time series on the number of tourist arrivals in the region is not available, the available indirect statistics and anecdotal evidence indicate that international tourist arrivals grew rapidly for several years prior to the outbreak of the COVID-19 pandemic. As noted earlier, the number of people passing the road BCPs between Sugd and Tashkent oblast increased 50 times between 2016 and 2019. During 2015–2018, international visitor arrivals in STKEC countries rose considerably—largely due to increased cross-border movement of people between Kazakhstan and Uzbekistan and between Tajikistan and Uzbekistan (Table 11). In 2018, Uzbekistan and Tajikistan were among the top four origin countries of international visitor arrivals in Kazakhstan. Likewise, Uzbekistan and Kazakhstan were among the top four origin countries of foreigners who visited Tajikistan, and Kazakhstan and Tajikistan were the top two origin countries of international visitor arrivals in Uzbekistan (Table 12).

Table 11: STKEC Countries—International Visitor Arrivals by Country of Origin, 2014–2018 ('000)

	2014	2015	2016	2017	2018
Kazakhstan					
From all countries	6,332.7	6,430.2	6,509.4	7,701.2	8,789.3
From Uzbekistan	2,107.2	2,297.2	2,459.8	3,344.6	4,351.3
From Tajikistan	137.4	158.5	207.0	383.4	142.5
Uzbekistan					
From all countries	1,938.0	2,034.3	2,157.7	2,847.9	6,433.0
From Kazakhstan	1,164.0	1,285.0	1,412.2	1,783.8	2,456.9
From Tajikistan	291.2	246.8	213.7	261.9	1,700.7
Tajikistan					
From all countries	197.3	401.1	330.9	410.9	1,020.8
From Kazakhstan	16.0	12.8	14.0	20.0	13.9
From Uzbekistan	74.5	106.1	12.5	101.0	733.2

STKEC = Shymkent–Tashkent–Khujand Economic Corridor.

Note: A large number of foreigners (particularly citizens of Uzbekistan and Tajikistan) visiting Kazakhstan are labor migrants working in Kazakhstan or transiting via Kazakhstan to the Russian Federation. Likewise, a substantial number of the citizens of Tajikistan visiting Uzbekistan are labor migrants transiting through Uzbekistan to Kazakhstan and the Russian Federation.

Sources: Statistics Committee of the Ministry of National Economy of the Republic of Kazakhstan, State Committee of the Republic of Uzbekistan on Statistics, and Government of the Republic of Tajikistan.

Table 12: STKEC Countries—Top 10 Origin Countries of International Visitor Arrivals, 2018

Rank	Kazakhstan	Uzbekistan	Tajikistan
1	Uzbekistan	Kazakhstan	Russian Federation
2	Russian Federation	Tajikistan	Uzbekistan
3	Kyrgyz Republic	Kyrgyz Republic	Kyrgyz Republic
4	Tajikistan	Russian Federation	Kazakhstan
5	Turkey	Turkmenistan	Belarus
6	Germany	Afghanistan	Armenia
7	Azerbaijan	Turkey	PRC
8	Belarus	PRC	Moldova
9	Ukraine	Republic of Korea	Turkmenistan
10	PRC	India	Ukraine

PRC = People's Republic of China, STKEC = Shymkent–Tashkent–Khujand Economic Corridor.

Source: United Nations World Tourism Organization. *Tourism Statistics*. https://www.e-unwto.org/toc/unwtotfb/current (accessed 13 February 2020).

As in other parts of the world, the COVID-19 pandemic had a major adverse impact on tourism in the STKEC region. All STKEC countries imposed travel restrictions and the number of international tourist arrivals in the region fell sharply in the first 4 months of 2020.

Prospects of the tourism industry. The near-term prospects of the tourism industry in this region chiefly depend on the COVID-19 situation in the region and the rest of the world. Its medium- and long-term prospects depend on many external and internal factors. The following internal factors will have a significant impact on the development of the industry in the medium to long term:

(i) image and perception among consumers in target markets and segments;

(ii) accessibility (availability, quality, and affordability of passenger transport services, visa requirements, and border-crossing arrangements);

(iii) quality of tourist facilities and services;

(iv) range and attractiveness of tourism products; and

(v) tourism education and training.

Image and brand perception. At present, most of the international visitor arrivals in the STKEC region are from other Commonwealth of Independent States (CIS) countries—that is, countries that share the common Soviet Union history and have many cultural and ethnic links with STKEC countries. Other large and growing tourism markets include the PRC, Turkey, and the Republic of Korea. To increase the number of visitors from existing markets and attract visitors from other markets, the region needs targeted marketing strategies and promotions. In the STKEC region, tourism marketing and branding are still at an early stage and many tourism assets are not widely known. Brochures of some tourist places are only in Russian (e.g., the Bahoriston Health Resort in Tajikistan), and tourism information (or comprehensive tour guiding, for example) is not easily obtained. Information on the characteristics of the tourism markets in the STKEC region is still lacking and the language barrier remains a key issue in raising the image of the region.

The international market needs a solid perception of the STKEC region as a collective tourism destination and of its cities and oblasts as independent attractions. Marketing efforts should present that the region (i) offers a range of outstanding tourism experiences with high-quality facilities and services, (ii) is easy to reach and travel in, and (iii) provides a safe and secure environment for travellers. Presenting a coherent, persuasive, and positive tourism image for the STKEC region remains a long-term goal. In the short to medium term, however, the focus can be on (i) establishing cooperation among the various stakeholders within the region, (ii) creating strong images and brands of the region, and (ii) developing joint tourism products and experiences to attract more visitors.

Given their geographical proximity, and the shared history and culture of cities and oblasts within the STKEC region, a well-designed regional brand and image with respective experiences can attract international tourists. The region's brand can focus on its historical and cultural heritage as part of the Silk Road, which can easily be recognized and appreciated by international travellers. For 2020, the travel experts at Lonely Planet chose the Central Asian part of the Silk Road as the best tourist destination—because of its stunning mosques and madrassahs, vibrant bazaars, beautiful scenery, and generous Central Asian hospitality.[62] However, research on the main target markets is required. This will identify what segment of international tourists can be targeted (e.g., CIS countries, the PRC, or other emerging markets), gauge current perceptions of the region, and test potential marketing concepts.

For this purpose, an overall STKEC tourism expert group for marketing can be institutionalized. This expert group must ensure a degree of consistency and compatibility in creating an image of the STKEC region—as a destination with an outstanding range of natural and cultural heritage resources not found in any part of the world, and with quality service standards. This expert group shall coordinate closely with the overall CAREC tourism expert group to ensure alignment with the overall marketing and branding pillar of the CAREC Tourism Strategy 2030 currently under development. The CAREC tourism web portal can also be used as a marketing tool to promote tourism in the STKEC region. The Greater Mekong Subregion (GMS) tourism marketing strategy provides insights on how this can be done (Box 4).

Box 4: Greater Mekong Subregion Tourism Marketing Strategy and Action Plan, 2015–2020

The Greater Mekong Subregion (GMS) Tourism Working Group developed the GMS Tourism Marketing Strategy and Action Plan, 2015–2020 to align the national tourism development plans of all six GMS countries and promote the GMS as a single tourism destination with diversified and integrated tourism offerings. The strategy establishes common ground and identifies opportunities for joint development among GMS countries to (i) boost multicountry visits and tourist spending, (ii) improve the business climate, (iii) strengthen market linkages, (iv) expand product distribution channels, and (v) attract private investments. The overall outcome of the strategy is increased GMS tourism industry competitiveness manifested by (i) an increase in the total number of international tourist arrivals, and (ii) improved position of GMS countries in the World Economic Forum Travel & Tourism Competitiveness Index.

Marketing approaches and activities, such as e-marketing and online promotion of the GMS, are being implemented. These include disseminating online information and special content through websites (e.g., ExperienceMekong.org and MekongTourism.org), and using newsletters and social media platforms (e.g., Facebook, Instagram, TripAdvisor, etc.). Each GMS country also identifies priority secondary destinations to include in travel promotions and organize special thematic events. Overall, these joint marketing efforts aim to promote a unique and well-known GMS tourism brand, promote diversified but linked tourist products, and support institutional cooperation among all countries in the subregion.

Source: Mekong Tourism. Experience Mekong Tourism Marketing Strategy, 2015–2020. https://www.mekongtourism.org/about/marketing-strategy/.

---

[62]   Advantour. 2019. Central Asian Silk Road Named the World's #1 Destination for Tourists in 2020. 28 October. https://www.advantour.com/tajikistan/news/20191028-14.htm.

Accessibility by air transport. There are airports in all three cities of Shymkent, Tashkent, and Khujand. Tashkent has the best air connectivity with the rest of the world, with nearly 20 airlines linking the city with different world destinations. Less than 10 airlines have flights to Shymkent and/or Khujand.

Many people from the outside find it inconvenient to travel to the STKEC region due to insufficient flight connections. Two problems stand out: the lack of direct flights and the low flight frequency. Thus, air connectivity must be improved to attract more international tourists. Opening the aviation market can stimulate tourism by increasing flight frequencies and reducing transport costs and travel time. Although developing the aviation industry requires large investments, in turn, it has the potential to stimulate tourism flows, expand the demand for aviation services, and allow investors a significant return on their investment. Improving air access in the STKEC region can be undertaken through a phased approach, as recommended in the CAREC Aviation Scoping Study.[63]

Accessibility by land transport. Given the short distances between the cities and oblasts, people can travel within the STKEC region by land transport. There are regular bus and passenger railway services between Shymkent and Tashkent cities, and between Turkestan and Tashkent cities. There are also regular bus services between Tashkent and Khujand cities. One of the issues in these public transport services is the long travel time, partly due to the long stops at BCPs. Another deficiency is, except in some cases, travel arrangements cannot be done through online platforms.

Visa requirements. STKEC countries grant each other's citizens a visa-free entry for visits up to 30 days but implement different visa regimes for visitors from other countries (Table 13). Uzbekistan has the most liberalized visa regime among the three countries. Beginning February 2019, it granted 30 day visa-free entry to 45 countries and added a 7-day visa-free entry to the PRC in January 2020. Kazakhstan grants visa-free entry to 73 countries for a stay of 30–90 days, and to Hong Kong, China for a stay of 14 days. Similarly, Tajikistan also grants visa-free entry for 30–90 days, albeit to only 10 countries. Visitors from non-visa exempt countries are required to secure visas from the relevant diplomatic missions. If no diplomatic missions are present in the countries of residence or origin, (such as the Philippines where STKEC countries have no diplomatic presence), visitors may obtain a visa-upon-arrival instead.

Table 13: Visa Entry Requirements in STKEC for Top 10 Inbound Countries, 2019

	Travelling to		
	Kazakhstan	Uzbekistan	Tajikistan
Russian Federation	F	F	F
Kyrgyz Republic	F	F	F
Turkmenistan	E	C	A[a]/E
Belarus	F	F	F
Azerbaijan	F	F	F
Ukraine	F	F	F
Turkey	F	F	A[a]/E
PRC	C	C	A[a]/E
Republic of Korea	F	F	C
Germany	F	F	A[a]/E

A = visa on arrival, C = visa required prior to travel, E = e-visa, F = visa-free, PRC = People's Republic of China, STKEC = Shymkent–Tashkent–Khujand Economic Corridor.

[a] only at Dushanbe Airport

Source: International Air Transport Association. Travel Centre. https://www.iatatravelcentre.com/ (accessed 17 February 2020).

---

[63] ADB and CAREC. 2018. *Aviation and the Role of CAREC: A Scoping Study.* Manila. https://www.adb.org/sites/default/files/publication/452736/aviation-role-carec-study.pdf.

Tourist-friendly visa procedures are among the key measures to attract more international tourists. One such procedure is the Silk Visa for Central Asia, a Schengen-style single tourist visa for entry to Kazakhstan and Uzbekistan. At the time of this writing, it is at an advanced stage of preparation. Once fully implemented, it will grant foreigners entry to both countries with only one joint visa. Moving forward, the Silk Visa can be expanded later to include Tajikistan (and the Kyrgyz Republic) so that travellers can explore the entire STKEC region without additional visa requirements.[64] Meanwhile, visas-on-arrival or online e-visas can improve convenience for international travellers. STKEC countries can establish uniform entry requirements that do not necessitate making in-person or e-mail applications ahead of travel. Dedicated lanes and other facilitating measures, such as common signages, can also be introduced for international tourists at immigration in airports and land borders.

Tourism facilities and services. Tourist facilities and services in the STKEC region are less than sufficient. A web search on tourism-related establishment and/or properties (e.g., accommodation, travel agency, food, and other services) reveal that tourism facilities are at various levels in sufficiency, with Tashkent city having the biggest number of tourism facilities (301), followed by Shymkent (53), and Khujand (15). Tourism facilities are scarce in Turkestan and Sugd oblasts, with a few or even no facilities found in some of the mountain resorts. Or facilities may also be available, but not found in a web search.

These findings also mirror the results of the TripAdvisor reviews for the top 10 attractions in Tashkent city, (4,064 review), Shymkent (167 reviews), and Khujand (212 reviews).[65] Tashkent is ranked highest as tourist destination, with Shymkent and Khujand being less popular as tourist destinations, suggesting a need for image improvement. Issues from the reviews include (i) language barriers, such as tourists who know Russian often find it easier to navigate the local transport (bus, taxi, metro) than those who do not; (ii) local transport issues, such as difficult to find fixed advertised prices for many destinations; and (iii) less than satisfactory experience with hotels (Table 14).

Table 14: Tourist Satisfaction Review of Shymkent, Tashkent, and Khujand Cities, 2019

Shymkent		Tashkent		Khujand	
Shymkent Plaza	●●●●◖ 13 reviews	Metro Tashkent	●●●●◖ 1,241 reviews	Kayrakkum Reservoir	●●●●◖ 29 reviews
Park Abaya	●●●● 51 reviews	Chorsu Bazaar	●●●● 596 reviews	Historical Local Lore Museum	●●●● 53 reviews
Central Park	●●●●◖ 11 reviews	Navoi Opera Theater	●●●●◖ 143 reviews	Arbob Cultural Palace	●●●● 10 reviews
Mall Mega	●●●◖ 13 reviews	Teleshayakh Mosque	●●●●● 247 reviews	Park Kamal Khudzhandi	●●●●◖ 14 reviews
Independence Park	●●●● 6 reviews	Uzbekistan State Museum of Applied Art	●●●●◖ 254 reviews	Khujand Fortress	●●●◖ 29 reviews
Museum of Victims of Political Suppressions	●●●◖ 19 reviews	Amir Timur Museum	●●●● 269 reviews	Masjidi Jami Mosque	●●●● 18 reviews
Yuzhno-Kazakhstanskiy Museum	●●●●◖ 4 reviews	Chimgon	●●●●◖ 247 reviews	Somoni Park	●●●● 28 reviews

continued on next page

continued on next page

---

[64]   This new initiative was announced at the March 2018 Summit of Heads of State of Central Asia, led by the governments of Kazakhstan and Uzbekistan. Modelled along the lines of European Union's Schengen visa arrangement, this would permit all Central Asian countries along the Silk Road to be visited on a single tourist visa. Advantages include (i) reducing the time for visa issuance to just 10–14 days and facilitating multicountry visits, (ii) clear and standard procedures for obtaining the visa, (iii) improving the safety of travellers by granting Silk Road visa tourists a special status, (iv) facilitating the organization of travel groups, and (v) support in developing new interregional routes involving two or more countries.

[65]   These surveys' grading scale is from 1–5 (lowest–highest). They offer perspectives on how tourists compare these destinations to others on common global standards. The weighted average score is calculated from the tourists' points given to the 10 most favorite attractions on TripAdvisor.

Table 14 *continued*

Shymkent		Tashkent		Khujand	
Shymkent Zoo	●●●◑ 16 reviews	Amir Timur Square	●●●● 452 reviews	House Museum Kamal Khudzhandi	●●●●◑ 8 reviews
Ontustik Tourism Center	●●●●◑ 5 reviews	Minor Mosque	●●●●◑ 150 reviews	Kamal Khudzhandi Statue	●●●●◑ 10 reviews
Ayna Bazaar	●●●● 1 review	Mustakillik Square	●●●● 465 reviews	Monument to Ismoil Somoni	●●●● 53 reviews
Weighted Ave. Score	**3.87**		**4.28**		**4.07**

Source: TripAdvisor. *Top Attractions*. https://www.tripadvisor.com/ (accessed 13 February 2020).

Like in other parts of the world, the near-term priority for the tourism industry in STKEC countries should be the adoption of enhanced health and safety standards and protocols. This will help STKEC countries revive their tourism industries while keeping COVID-19 under control. In the medium to long term, the three countries will need to upgrade many existing tourism facilities, establish new facilities, and improve the quality of services (e.g., tourist information and travel services) to spur the development of the industry. Developing common tourism standards and setting up a shared certification system could help establish the STKEC region as a strong tourism destination for different kinds of travellers. Association of Southeast Asian Nations (ASEAN) Community-Based Tourism Standard, which covers the full range of tourism operations and service, can be a model for STKEC regional tourism development (Box 5).

Box 5: ASEAN Community-Based Tourism Standard

The Association of Southeast Asian Nations (ASEAN) established the Community-Based Tourism (CBT) Standard in 2016 as a common benchmark of performance for tourism businesses in ASEAN member countries to assure visitors of good and meaningful experiences, and communities of sustainable and mutual benefits from tourism activities. This standard—consistent with the 10 CBT Principles pertaining to the ownership, management, product and service quality, benefits sharing, and sustainability of local tourism industries—cover the following eight areas:

- community ownership and management,
- contribution to social well-being,
- conservation and improvement of the environment,
- interaction between the local and community guests,
- quality of tour and guiding services,
- quality of food and beverage services,
- quality of accommodations, and
- performance of (inbound) CBT-friendly tour operators.

Tourism activities that comply with the applicable criteria, performance indicators, and codes of conduct operationalizing the standard can be certified as CBT initiatives. To be certified, tour operators must have trained and skilled staff, responsible marketing to manage client expectations, and effective feedback mechanisms to improve the quality of their operations. Businesses are also prescribed to help fund community development activities, build capacities of disadvantaged community members, and facilitate benefit-sharing agreements.

Generally, a CBT certification signals commitment to deliver value to tourist markets and ensure the collective well-being of communities by promoting local livelihoods, conserving natural and cultural resources, and encouraging equitable interactions.

Source: ASEAN Secretariat. 2016. ASEAN Community-Based Tourism Standard. Jakarta. https://www.asean.org/storage/2012/05/ASEAN-Community-Based-Tourism-Standard.pdf.

Roadside services. Roadside service pertains to gas stations, parking spaces, service centers (e.g., restaurants, rest areas, shops), accommodations (e.g., hotels, motels), and emergency road assistance services and facilities, among others, which help ensure the safety and comfort of road travelers. These services facilitate smoother and more convenient road travel, encouraging more tourism and trade. Roadside infrastructure services across the STKEC countries are inadequate and their quality can still be vastly improved.

Available information on Kazakhstan indicates that of the 1,822 roadside service facilities in the country, only 865 (47%) meet the national standard. Similarly, in the Turkestan oblast, 363 facilities (almost 70%) of the 529 roadside service facilities do not meet the national standard—characterized by inadequate parking and low quality of services. There is, therefore, a strong need to reconstruct and install more sanitary facilities and increase accommodation facilities.

Tourism products. The STKEC region has many tourist assets to attract international travelers. Table 15 summarizes the results of a web search of tourism attractions and core tourism products in the Kazakh, Uzbek, and Tajik parts of the region.

Table 15: Major Tourist Attractions and Tourism Products in the STKEC Region

Tourism Areas	Tourist Attractions	Core Tourism Products
Shymkent city and Turkestan oblast	• Mausoleum of Khoja Ahmed Yasawi • Arystan Bab Mausoleum • Intimate Ruins of Sauran • Archaeological Site of Otrar • Aksu-Zhabagly Nature Reserve	• Culture and architecture • Religious tourism • Nature and adventure (trekking, bicycle riding, etc.) • City break (shopping)
Tashkent city and Tashkent oblast	• Charvak Reservoir • Amir Timur Museum • Minor Mosque • Teleshayakh Mosque • Kukeldash Madrasah • Chorsu Bazaar • Chimgan Ski Resort • Navoi Park	• Culture and architecture • Religious tourism • Nature and adventure (skiing, trekking, bicycle riding, etc.) • City break (shopping) • Business (meetings, conventions, and exhibitions)
Sugd oblast	• Kayrakkum Reservoir • Fortress Mug Teppe • Historical Local Lore Museum of Archeology and Fortification • Medressa of Abdullatif Sultan • Iskanderkul Lake • Zeravshan Valley • Panjshanbe Market • Masjidi Jami Mosque • Arbob Cultural Palace	• Culture and architecture • Nature and adventure (trekking, bicycle riding, etc.) • City break (shopping)

STKEC = Shymkent–Tashkent–Khujand Economic Corridor.

Source: TripAdvisor. 2020. *Top Attractions.* https://www.tripadvisor.com/.

The CAREC Tourism Scoping Study identified a range of tours offered from European source countries to CAREC countries (including STKEC countries). These include (i) tours following sections of the Silk Road; (ii) nature-based tours—mainly hard adventure (e.g., trekking and winter sports); (iii) combined cultural heritage and nature sightseeing tours; and (iv) city tours. Table 16 is a summary of the multicountry tour programs offered, which include at least two of the three STKEC countries.

Table 16: Multicountry Tour Programs Offered from Europe to STKEC Countries

☐ Non-STKEC country included   ☐ STKEC country included

Tour	Countries					Days
Silk Road and Other Historical Tours						
Silk Road Tour of Central Asia by Kalpak Travel	KAZ	UZB	TAJ	KGZ		15
Various Tours by Mircorp	KAZ	TKM	UZB	TAJ	KGZ	14–16
Silk Road Tours by Avantour	KAZ	TKM	UZB	TAJ	PRC	19
Adventure Tours						
Ultimate Fann Mountain Trek by KE Adventour Travel	UZB	TAJ				15
Combined Historical, Cultural, and Nature Heritage Tours						
Best of Central Asia by Avantour, Evaneos	TKM	UZB	TAJ	KGZ		8–27
Mountains and Marvels of Central Asia by KE Adventour Travel	KAZ	TKM	UZB	TAJ	KGZ	15

KAZ = Kazakhstan, KGZ = Kyrgyz Republic, PRC = People's Republic of China, STKEC = Shymkent–Tashkent–Khujand Economic Corridor, TAJ = Tajikistan, TKM = Turkmenistan, UZB = Uzbekistan.
Sources: Websites of tour operators (accessed 17 February 2020).

As shown by this Google search results, the present range of tours offered in STKEC countries involve two broad market segments: those with deep interest and commitment to hard adventure experiences, and those with a fascination for the Silk Road and associated historic and cultural heritage features. These broad tourism demands coincide well with the tourism endowment of the STKEC region. Given these clear and sufficient demands for tourism, what is critical is how to fulfill these demands in an effective way. Thus, to realize their full tourism potential, one of the challenges for STKEC countries is how to develop new tourism products that could offer a broad range of joint and combined tours.

These new products should be tailored to the specific needs and preferences of different segments of the tourism market. Under the broad brand of the Silk Road, tour packages can be developed based on STKEC region's unique set of tourism assets and their potential for development. Tour packages can comprise (i) purely of historical and cultural sites, religious site visits, city tours, or nature attractions; or (ii) any combination of these destinations. These packages can also differ in length or duration, and types of activities to meet the different tastes and demands of tourists. These packages can even include other tourist attractions outside the STKEC region (e.g., Samarkand) or other countries (e.g., the Kyrgyz Republic) to increase their appeal. This will need extensive coordination among tour operators and governments of the concerned countries.

Tourism policies and strategies of STKEC countries are focused on (i) expanding the range and upgrading their respective tourism products to reach a broader market; (ii) creating thematic clusters of tourism products to achieve a certain scope and quality that appeal to tourists; (iii) spreading the socioeconomic benefits from tourism development to the STKEC countries and the region; and (iv) creating year-round tourism experiences to maintain demand through all the seasons. Some joint products and programs are already being developed. The "Tourism Ring of Central Asia" and "In the Footsteps of Tamerlan" are examples of joint tourism programs that were initiated by the private sector.

Nature and adventure tours. The STKEC region has rich natural landscapes with unique mountains and lakes. These sites can be developed and promoted to tourists from within and outside the region who wish to enjoy short or long stays for skiing, trekking, bicycling, and other outdoor or recreational activities. Setting a uniform standard for facilities and services, and undertaking joint marketing are key areas for regional cooperation. Establishing a joint tourism association among the various operators in the region, which the European Association of Mountain Areas (Euromontana) has done, may be a good example to follow (Box 6).

Box 6: European Association of Mountain Areas (Euromontana)

In Europe, tourists increasingly choose to go to the mountains for the holidays. The influx of tourists raises questions about the environmental implications of increased tourism and the capacity of regions to accommodate and provide the right infrastructure to support the industry. The challenge, therefore, is adapting to meet the growing demand and broadening accessibility while offering sustainable tourism activities.

In line with this, Euromontana, a "multisectoral association for co-operation and development of mountain territories" in the greater European area, identifies the following best practices:

- **Sustainable mountain tourism activities.** The "Espubike" project in Spain stimulates the local economy without negatively impacting the natural and cultural heritage of the area as its 146-kilometer cycling trail allows visitors to traverse some of the protected areas of the Regional Park of Sierra Espuña, as well as the nearby villages.

- **Energy efficiency in mountain hotels.** The Cyprianerhof Hotel near the Rosengarten massif in South Tyrol, Italy reduces costs, minimizes waste, and saves energy while providing a healthy and comfortable environment for its guests by implementing various ecology-oriented initiatives. These include using locally sourced materials and produce to support hotel operations, encouraging guests to minimize their own wastes, and maintaining an energy management system (e.g., use of LED lights, adjustment to lower electric currents, and regular energy audit to identify areas for improvement).

- **Improved accessibility of mountain destinations.** The "Trentino Accessible" initiative successfully implemented measures to improve the region's accessibility for disabled tourists. It developed a mobile application and "Ibus Voice" to deliver auditory information to tourists with disabilities. It also partnered with Euromontana for the Silver Tourism project where tours are developed around the needs and interests of older people.

Source: European Association of Mountain Areas. 2017. Mountain Tourism: Do You Know These Good Practices?" https://www.euromontana.org/en/tourism-in-mountain-do-you-know-these-good-practices/.

Culture and leisure tourism. The tour packages could include (i) major historical and/or religious sites, city tours, cultural heritage sites, and nature sites, with different lengths or durations; or (ii) a combination of different tourist sites and activities to meet different tastes and demands of tourists. Tour packages can be expanded to include tourist attractions outside the STKEC region (e.g., Samarkand) and other countries (e.g., the Kyrgyz Republic) to increase the appeal of these tours. These will need the seamless cooperation and collaboration among all the tour operators and governments of these countries. The experiences of the Classic Baltic Group Tour among Lithuania, Latvia, and Estonia can be applied when developing such a program in the STKEC region (Box 7).

Box 7: Classic Baltic Group Tour: Lithuania, Latvia, and Estonia

The Classic Baltic Group Tour offered by the Baltic Travel Services is a 5-day tour covering three countries—Lithuania, Latvia, and Estonia. It is one of the most top-rated tours on TripAdvisor, having a rating of 5 stars from 83 reviews. The tour is conducted in English and is most popular among clients from Europe.

Day 1: Tourists arrive in Vilnius, the largest city and the capital of Lithuania. They enjoy a private guided tour of the historic Vilnius Old Town and the Trakai Castle in Trakai, another historic city and lake resort in Lithuania. They return to Vilnius and spend the rest of the evening there.

Day 2: Tourists leave Vilnius for Riga, the capital of Latvia. On the way, tourists are treated to a short side trip to the famous Hill of Crosses near Siauliai. The trip from Vilnius to Riga takes approximately 5 hours by bus. Once in Riga, tourists enjoy a private walking tour through Riga Old Town, which includes the Riga Castle founded in 1330, the Parliament, the Monument of Liberty, and the Opera House. After that, tourists are free to spend the rest of the evening in Riga as they please.

Day 3: Tourists go on a guided private tour of the Art Nouveau District in Riga, renowned for its architecture. Then, they see the attractions in Sigulda, a town less than an hour's drive away from Riga, which is known for its historic monuments and natural landscape. They return to Riga in the afternoon and spend the rest of the evening there.

Day 4: Tourists travel approximately 4.5 hours by bus to Tallinn, the capital city of Estonia. They tour the Tallinn Old Town, a United Nations Educational, Scientific and Cultural Organization heritage site. Afterward, they visit Toompea Hill and Toompea Castle built during the 13th–14th centuries, which now serves as the seat of Estonia's Parliament. Tourists spend the rest of the evening in Tallinn.

Day 5: Tourists are free to go around the city as they please before their transfer schedule to Tallinn International Airport, where they depart for home or their next destination.

Source: TripAdvisor. 2020. Attractions. https://www.tripadvisor.com.ph/Attraction_Review-g274967-d10072603-Reviews-Baltic-Travel_Services-Riga_Riga_Region.html.

Medical and health tourism. Promoting medical tourism in the STKEC region has the potential to yield great benefits for both STKEC and other foreign countries. Medical tourism between Shymkent and Tashkent has been a long-standing practice. Informal sources indicate that over 1,000 people from Shymkent seek medical treatment in Tashkent every year because of the latter's comparatively lower cost and better quality of medical services and equipment, strong knowledge base, and historical background in medicine since the former Soviet Union era. Medical institutions in Tashkent offer services, such as therapeutic examinations and treatment, diagnosis, magnetic resonance imaging, laparoscopies, and ultrasounds. Other services include cardiosurgical, neurosurgical, dental care, as well as natural therapies (with some nature places in Uzbekistan being used for specific medical purposes). Apart from the medical care, the conveniences of geographic proximity, shared history, and common language make it desirable for Shymkent citizens to seek medical treatment in Tashkent.

Medical tourism and nature-based therapy and treatment in the STKEC region can be better developed and coordinated by standardizing services and complying with international certifications. The initial target markets can be countries of the former Soviet Union, then gradually expand its coverage to other countries. Best practices in medical tourism can be derived from the experience of some Southeast Asian countries. Singapore, for example, has a well-developed medical tourism industry because of its state-of-the-art facilities and highly specialized medical services, such as in oncology and cardiology. Meanwhile, Malaysia and Thailand are actively promoting medical tourism by developing special medical tourism packages for foreign patients where assistance includes arranging accommodations, obtaining a visa, and organizing transport such as airport pickups and drop-offs.

Hence, medical tourists can benefit not only from their excellent health-care system, but also enjoy the services with greater ease.[66]

Business and event tourism. Business and event tourism is globally an emerging driver for tourism sector development. This type of tourism can (i) create opportunities for knowledge-sharing and innovation that could help local economies, (ii) raise the international profile of the host country, and (iii) provide venues for networking, among others.[67] Engaging in business and event tourism may be advantageous individually for the STKEC countries and collectively for the region. Tashkent is already well known as a host country in Central Asia because of its well-established infrastructure (e.g., metro system) and track record for hosting local, regional, and international events. While Shymkent is gaining momentum in hosting international events, Khujand has a large untapped potential. To boost business and event tourism, the region can capitalize on its tourism attractions, improved connectivity, proximity to each other, and warmer climate that is favorable to tourists throughout the year.

Tourism education and training. As tourism assumes an increasing role in the economy of STKEC countries, an adequate supply of qualified tourism officials and managers—trained in planning and implementation—will be needed to achieve the region's full tourism potential. They can be initially educated through cooperation with overseas institutions but, eventually, local universities should be providing the necessary education.

Developments in tourism education and cooperation among STKEC countries are promising. The Silk Road International Tourism University in Samarkand started offering tourism courses in 2018. In 2019, the university signed a memorandum for the exchange of faculty, staff, and students with the Kazakhstan International University of Tourism and Hospitality for the purpose of training, research, and exchange of experience. Moving forward, this kind of cooperation can also be extended to universities in Tajikistan.[68]

Tourism staff need to be equipped with technical, linguistic, and social skills, including information and communication technology (ICT) skills. Technical and linguistic skills can be taught through common curricula based on international systems, and those who qualify must secure certifications. This will ensure that high-quality services are provided to tourists and are consistent with international standards. However, social skills can only be partly taught. Service providers in the tourism industry should be allowed to express their own character and differentiate their brand of service from other destinations. For a more regional approach to tourism education and training, programs can be established in each country using a common curricula and certification system. Students from two or more countries can be trained and taught together to encourage understanding, cooperation, and exchange of ideas. STKEC countries would greatly benefit from a regional approach not only in developing enhanced health and safety standards and protocols for the tourism industry, but also in building the capacity of tourism establishments to implement these standards and protocols. Such a regional approach could include a joint online training program in enhanced health and safety standards and protocols.

Planned and/or proposed actions. Based on the analysis presented in the earlier sections, a series of proposed actions are summarized in Table 17. These are divided into the following seven broad categories: (i) accessibility, (ii) tourism infrastructure and services, (iii) tourism products and experiences, (iv) marketing and promotion, (v) tourism skills and services, (vi) financing and other support, and (vii) organization and institution.

---

[66] help@wotmed.com. 2019. *10 Best Countries for Medical Tourism.* https://wotmed.com/blog-10-best-countries-for-medical-tourism/.

[67] *TTGMice.* 2017. The Growing Importance of Business Events to Local Tourism Industry. 4 May. https://www.ttgmice.com/2017/05/04/the-growing-importance-of-business-events-to-local-tourism-industry/.

[68] *UZ Daily.* 2019. Silk Road International Tourism University and Kazakhstan Tourism University Signed a Memorandum of Cooperation. 23 December. https://uzdaily.uz/en/post/53828.

Table 17: Planned and Proposed Actions to Develop Regional Tourism

Category	Actions
Accessibility	• Harmonize the STKEC countries' visa regimes for international visitors. • Simplify further the visa application procedures for international visitors (through greater use of digital technologies and issuance of visas-on-arrival at more BCPs). • Expedite the introduction of the Silk Visa—a single tourist visa for entry to Kazakhstan and Uzbekistan—and expand the coverage of the Silk Visa to include Tajikistan and other countries. • Rehabilitate secondary and tertiary roads to enable access to tourism sites, including tourism sites in the STKEC region. • Conduct a feasibility study to develop roads and other infrastructure, which are needed to connect recreational tourism sites in the eastern part of Turkestan oblast with those in the northern part of Tashkent oblast. • Implement the recommendations of the CAREC Aviation Scoping Study to improve air transport connectivity to and from the STKEC region.
Tourism infrastructure and services	• Develop enhanced health and safety standards and protocols for the tourism industry and ensure that all tourism establishments implement these standards and protocols. • Increase the number of tourism information centers. • Improve tourism signage. • Build and/or improve roadside infrastructure and services (e.g., sanitary facilities). • Build more tourism facilities (e.g., hotels, restaurants) in tourism site. • Upgrade existing tourism facilities to international standards. • Establish and implement certification schemes for the different types of tourism facilities.
Tourism products and experiences	• Develop diversified joint tour packages and programs that include major tourism sites and attractions across the region and operate on a pilot basis. • Increase existing tourism activities (e.g., leisure, business, and events), and expand health wellness tourism in the region. • Strengthen coordination in jointly developing tourism products and experiences among tourism associations and operators in Central Asia. • Establish and implement a certification for medical and health, and event tourism products under a single STKEC or Central Asia tourism umbrella and/or brand.
Marketing and promotion	• Establish an STKEC tourism support database to strengthen the collection and sharing of tourism statistics and market knowledge. • Create destination image and branding for the STKEC region under an overarching Silk Road marketing theme. • Conduct a joint market research on targeted tourism segments and markets. • Strengthen collaboration with the World Tourism Organization's (UNWTO) Silk Road Programme and the United Nations Educational, Scientific and Cultural Organization (UNESCO) for a joint market research on UNESCO-designated sites and natural and cultural heritage—for creating destination image and branding. • Strengthen coordination among marketing and promotion associations and operators in Central Asia. • Formulate an STKEC region-wide tourism marketing strategy.
Tourism skills and services	• Continue tourism education cooperation among universities and other education institutions (e.g., staff and faculty exchange). • Establish a joint online training program in enhanced health and safety standards and protocols for the tourism industry. • Develop common standards for tourism education and training courses at both national and regional levels. • Establish a region-wide certificate for tourism education programs.

continued on next page

Table 17 *continued*

Category	Actions
Financing and other support	• Continue to develop the project concepts of identified project proposals for possible funding by development partners and countries. • Develop a regional investment framework for foreign and local investors. • Identify funding mechanisms to accelerate project conceptualization and marketing of STKEC—to be financed through sovereign lending, nonsovereign lending, and technical assistance projects.
Organization and institution	• Institutionalize cooperation among tourism associations in Central Asia to develop regional approaches for tourism. • Establish an STKEC tourism expert group to advance tourism cooperation and improve public–private coordination and collaboration. • Develop a detailed STKEC tourism action plan under the overall framework of the CAREC tourism strategy.

BCP = border crossing point, CAREC = Central Asia Regional Economic Cooperation, STKEC = Shymkent–Tashkent–Khujand Economic Corridor.

Source: Asian Development Bank.

ADB and other development partners can provide technical assistance (TA) to help STKEC countries carry out these actions. The TA projects should be determined through consultations with government authorities and tourist experts in the region.

Regional initiatives could be implemented in partnership with international and bilateral development organizations and/or programs, such as the World Tourism Organization (UNWTO), United Nations Educational, Scientific and Cultural Organization (UNESCO), the Silk Road Fund, the EU, and other lending institutions and donors. Such collaborations could include (i) supporting and building synergies with the UNESCO and EU project on Silk Road Heritage Corridors in Afghanistan, Central Asia, and Iran; (ii) promoting cultural and natural heritage tourism in the STKEC region by drawing on UNESCO and UNWTO's experience in working with journalists and the travel industry; (iii) undertaking research on UNESCO-designated sites to guide destination image and branding development for the STKEC region; and (iv) undertaking market research in partnership with organizations, such as TripAdvisor.

4.6   Development of Special Economic Zones and Industrial Zones

A key feature of an economic corridor is its ability to attract investment through existing and/or planned economic nodes including special economic zones (SEZs) and industrial zones.[69] The final outcome of an economic corridor development depends—to a considerable degree—on the success of SEZs and industrial zones in integrating regional and global value chains and promoting cluster-based economic development along and beyond the corridor.

Special economic zones and industrial zones in the STKEC region. There are eight SEZs in the STKEC region (Figure 8).[70] A number of industrial zones also exist in the region. Among these SEZs and industrial zones are (i) manufacturing SEZs and industrial zones, (ii) an agro-industrial complex, (iii) a tourism SEZ, (iv) a fishing SEZ, and (v) a city-like SEZ.

---

[69] Industrial zones are a tract of land developed and subdivided into plots, according to a comprehensive plan, with a provision for roads, transport, and public utilities with or without factory buildings for the use of industrial enterprises. SEZs are a type of industrial zones where commercial activities are carried out under special regulatory, incentive, and institutional regimes that are different from the rest of the economy.

[70] In Tajikistan and Uzbekistan, SEZs are referred to as free economic zones.

Figure 8: Special Economic Zones in the STKEC Region

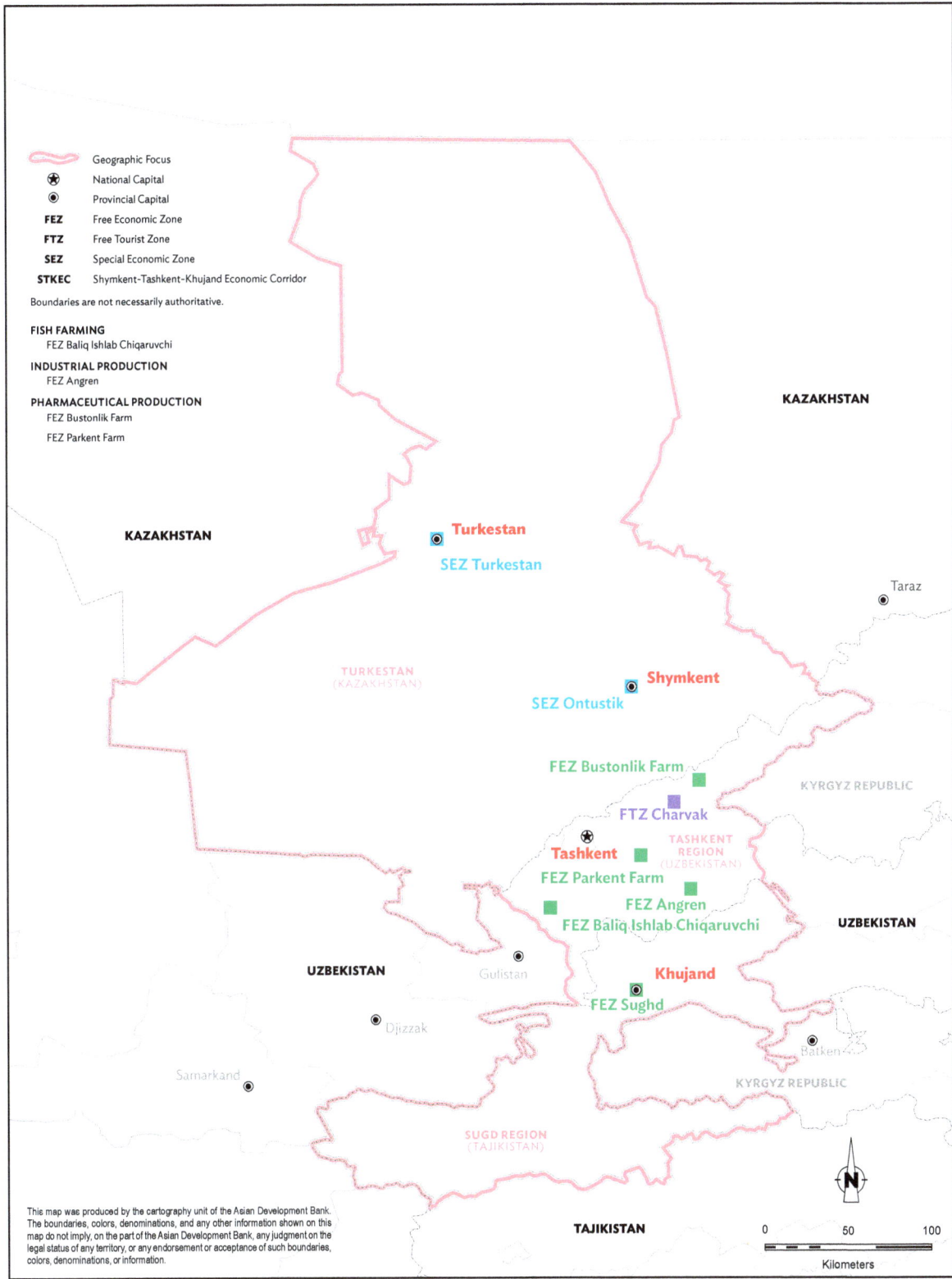

Geographic Focus
National Capital
Provincial Capital
FEZ Free Economic Zone
FTZ Free Tourist Zone
SEZ Special Economic Zone
STKEC Shymkent-Tashkent-Khujand Economic Corridor

Boundaries are not necessarily authoritative.

FISH FARMING
FEZ Baliq Ishlab Chiqaruvchi

INDUSTRIAL PRODUCTION
FEZ Angren

PHARMACEUTICAL PRODUCTION
FEZ Bustonlik Farm
FEZ Parkent Farm

KAZAKHSTAN

KAZAKHSTAN

Turkestan
SEZ Turkestan

TURKESTAN
(KAZAKHSTAN)

Taraz

Shymkent
SEZ Ontustik

FEZ Bustonlik Farm

KYRGYZ REPUBLIC

FTZ Charvak

TASHKENT
REGION
(UZBEKISTAN)

Tashkent
FEZ Parkent Farm

FEZ Angren
FEZ Baliq Ishlab Chiqaruvchi

UZBEKISTAN

UZBEKISTAN

Gulistan

Khujand
FEZ Sughd

Djizzak

Batken

KYRGYZ REPUBLIC

Samarkand

SUGD REGION
(TAJIKISTAN)

N

This map was produced by the cartography unit of the Asian Development Bank.
The boundaries, colors, denominations, and any other information shown on this
map do not imply, on the part of the Asian Development Bank, any judgment on the
legal status of any territory, or any endorsement or acceptance of such boundaries,
colors, denominations, or information.

TAJIKISTAN

0   50   100

Kilometers

201009D ABV

STKEC = Shymkent–Tashkent–Khujand Economic Corridor.

Source: Asian Development Bank.

(i)   **Manufacturing special economic zones and industrial zones.** There are five manufacturing SEZs of varying sizes in the STKEC region. These are (i) SEZ Ontustik in Shymkent; (ii) free economic zone (FEZ) Sugd in Khujand; and (iii) FEZs Angren, Bustonlik Farm, and Parkent Farm in Tashkent. While Sugd and Angren FEZs are multisectoral, Ontustik, Bustonlik Farm, and Parkent Farm are specialized. Ontustik focuses on textile and clothing and chemical and petrochemical industries; Bustonlik and Parkent farms are dedicated to the pharmaceutical industry. Both Sugd and Angren host wide-ranging industries—from textile to machinery, food to construction materials, to chemicals and electronics. The manufacturing SEZs are complemented by several manufacturing industrial zones in the Kazakh and Uzbek parts of the STKEC region (Tajikistan does not develop industrial zones). The Tashkent oblast alone hosts a cluster of 31 small industrial zones. In Shymkent city, there are two industrial zones—Ontustik and Tassey. These zones host small and medium-sized enterprises producing miscellaneous products. A new industrial zone—IZ Zhuldyz—and an agro-industrial zone are in the pipeline in Shymkent. There are also plans to expand SEZ Ontustik in both area and scope by including pharmaceutical as one of the target industries. The Turkestan region has nine industrial zones. These zones attract investment in construction and other industrial sectors. There are also plans to develop two industrial parks within SEZ Turkestan.

(ii)   **Agro-industrial complex.** Turkestan oblast promotes an agro-industrial complex, which complements the development of (i) agricultural production (poultry, livestock, and fishery); (ii) agricultural technologies; (iii) intermediate inputs (fertilizers, seeds, pesticides, and other high-yielding variety crops); (iv) implements (machines and other tools); (v) processing; and (vi) marketing—all in an integrated framework.

(iii)   **Tourism special economic zone.** Charvak is a tourism-based SEZ in Uzbekistan. Located in a mountainous part of Tashkent oblast, it is being developed as a destination for ecology and recreational tourism. SEZ Turkestan also has plans to develop a historical and religious center to position itself as a religious and cultural hub of Central Asia.

(iv)   **Fishing special economic zone.** FEZ "Baliq ishlab chiqaruvchi" was designed to develop a fish culture in Kuyichirchik district of Tashkent oblast—for promoting modern fish processing complexes.

(v)   **City-like special economic zone.** The SEZ Turkestan aims to accelerate the development of Turkestan city. In addition to the historical and religious center to enhance its tourism potential, it has four other subzones: an administrative business center, two industrial zones, and an airport with ambitious investment and employment targets.

One notes the clustering of a variety of SEZs and industrial zones within the region. These SEZs and industrial zones can draw strength and reinforce each other to develop a growth pole in the STKEC region.

Performance of special economic zones. Although information was limited, various sources indicate that the three major manufacturing SEZs in the STKEC region are Ontustik (Shymkent), Sugd (Khujand), and Angren (Tashkent) and were among the best-performing operational zones in their respective countries. SEZ Ontustik is the most efficient zone, which in 2019 attracted T15.5 of private investments per T1 budget—as against the average of a mere T2.9 per T1 budget. It is also the best performing in terms of employment, production, and exports (Table 18). Similarly, Sugd stood out in Tajikistan in terms of the number of projects, employment, and production per hectare (ha) of land (Table 19). Angren has a larger number of residents than the other operational zones, Navoi and Jizzakh, and in 2018, it outperformed them in terms of investment and foreign direct investment (FDI). However, despite being relatively better than the other SEZs in their respective countries, the three SEZs cannot be labeled "successful" in absolute terms. In Tajikistan, for instance, the 75 projects that SEZs attracted created a mere 1,095 jobs on 1,422 ha of land allocated to them—which means that less than one job was generated per ha of land. Even in Sugd FEZ, which is the best performing FEZ in the country, only 110 ha of land is occupied, while the rest (211 ha) remain vacant. Similarly, most zones have attracted low to medium technology-intensive activities and are dominated by domestic investment, which contributed 70% of total investment, as shown by the data from Kazakhstan and Uzbekistan.

Table 18: Performance of Selected Special Economic Zones in Kazakhstan: Selected Indicators, 2016

	Number of Jobs/ha	Investment ($ '000/ha)	Production ($ '000/ha)	Exports ($ '000/ha)	FDI ($ '000/ha)
SEZ Taraz	0.30	29.2	0.0	0.0	0.0
SEZ Saryarka	0.84	133.9	58.2	14.6	32.7
SEZ Pavlodar	0.34	35.5	5.6	0.4	1.3
SEZ NIPT	0.13	170.9	1.0	0.6	8.9
SEZ Ontustik	4.88	400.5	103.7	29.6	30.2

FDI = foreign direct investment, ha = hectare, NIPT = National Industrial Petrochemical Technopark, SEZ = special economic zone.

Sources: Official websites of each SEZ and consultations with representatives of the SEZs and Ministry of Industry and Infrastructural Development of Kazakhstan.

Table 19: Performance of Free Economic Zones in Tajikistan: Selected Indicators, 2019

	Number of projects/ha	Employment/ha	Production ($ '000/ha)	Investment ($ '000/ha)
Sugd	0.09	1.87	50.84	24.98
Dangara	0.05	0.78	7.06	341.73
Panj	0.04	0.13	0.20	4.08
Ishkoshim	0.03	0.07	0.02	1.95
National	0.05	0.74	13.93	130.43

ha = hectare.

Source: Ministry of Economic Development and Transport, Government of the Republic of Tajikistan. 2020. *Activity of Free Economic Zones of the Republic of Tajikistan.* http://fez.tj/eng/lastnews/196-activity-of-free-economic-zones-of-the-republic-of-tajikistan.html.

Overall, the SEZs or industrial zones in STKEC countries have failed to generate substantial gains. Therefore, it is crucial to dig deeper and understand the institutional contexts in which these zones are designed and administered. These contexts are shaped by a three-layered framework of investment climatic factors: micro, meso, and macro climatic factors.

Micro climatic factors. Micro climatic factors refer to the investment climate prevailing in the SEZs and industrial zones. These factors reflect "doing business" conditions, including the legal and institutional framework, incentives offered, one-stop-shop, and infrastructure created in these zones. In this region, the major strengths of micro climatic factors in the SEZs are (i) distinct legal frameworks; (ii) special legal regime in terms of tax, custom, labor, and currency; (iii) liberal tax breaks; and most importantly, (iv) strong political commitment to promote them.

However, challenges (or weaknesses) remain. First, the institutional structure, particularly of SEZs, is characterized by the same political economy of command, regulation, and centralized planning that characterize the outside economy in these countries. The STKEC countries have adopted an extremely cautious approach to reforming the SEZs. The underlying objective of attracting FDI through SEZs is to build competitiveness in import-substituting industries, but this may have been precluded by the small size of the domestic markets of the STKEC countries. While these SEZs offer an almost zero-tax regime, they score very low on the single window mechanism, the reliability of utilities (water, gas, and electricity), and the quality of infrastructure. The SEZs provide only the basic industrial infrastructure and not enough for (i) business development (e.g., common business facilities, exhibition facilities, or banking); (ii) specialized infrastructure (water treatment plant or effluent treatment plant); (iii) sector-specific infrastructure (e.g., testing facilities, common logistics centers, training centers, and others); and (iv) social infrastructure (e.g., residential complexes, malls, hotels, health facilities, recreational facilities, or shopping centers in or around SEZs). Electricity shortages pose a major bottleneck in some SEZs. Industrial zones do not have as much budgetary support as SEZs, hence, these are even more vulnerable even if they enjoy greater flexibilities.

Meso factors. Meso factors comprise regional capabilities—such as networks of specialized firms and service providers; connectivity to markets and gateways; and human skills, start-ups, and consortia that create an ecosystem to developing and upgrading the industry. From this perspective, a major strength of SEZs in the STKEC region is that they benefit from the proximity of the cities, which are major commercial and administrative centers of their respective countries. Regional development initiatives could bring new opportunities and improve the business climatic conditions in the STKEC region. For instance, in 2018, Shymkent—by the Decree of the President of Kazakhstan—was given the status of "the city of national significance," which drives the city to develop into a regional hub and a magnet for investors. A new Turkestan oblast was also created with an administrative center in Turkestan city. This is expected to create opportunities for investment and tourist growth and provide a major boost to industrial zones. In Tajikistan, the government's National Development Strategy 2030 highlights the need to shift from a primary sector-driven economy to an industrial economy. One of the key priorities of the Sugd oblast is to connect the north–east industrial areas of Khujand by railway, and create a logistics transport and trade center to provide a full range of trade and transport logistics services. There are also plans to transform Khujand into an entertainment and tourist site by developing the rural areas, along with tourism and folk crafts. In Tashkent city, there has been a massive modernization drive since 2017. Tashkent city alone attracted 21.7% of total fixed investment in Uzbekistan in 2016, compared with 2.5% in Jizzakh and 5.0% in Navoi. These regional initiatives are expected to generate economic momentum in the region and give a major boost to economic zones. STKEC countries also have natural advantages in agriculture, which offer immense opportunity for developing agro-industrial zones and/or complexes. The location of the STKEC region on the ancient Silk Road route, the rich historical and cultural heritage, natural sites, and availability of thermal waters provide great opportunities for developing different types of tourism packages. All these potentials could be tapped through the economic zones in the region. However, these remain untapped due to major constraints that characterize the zones' meso climatic conditions. These constraints include poor internal connectivity, poor conditions of internal roads, weak meso infrastructure, shortage of energy, and poor border crossing facilities. Transit trade between Kazakhstan and Uzbekistan has been growing rapidly but long delays occur at BCPs. The throughput capacity of the BCPs is very weak and needs to be improved from both sides (e.g., new driveways must be built, security checkpoints must be installed, and so on). In addition to the infrastructure constraints, there are challenges in the quality and effectiveness of the institutions, human capital, product markets, financial systems, and innovations. The STKEC provides an opportunity to address some of these meso climatic constraints by improving connectivity and trade facilitation.

Macro climatic factors. At the macro level, new opportunities are emerging that can be optimized for the development of SEZs and/or industrial zones. All three countries have been proactively implementing economic reforms with the aim of improving their investment climate. Further, governments in all three countries have developed dynamic industrialization strategies and taken several measures to implement them, including tax and financial incentives, introduction of investment laws to protect foreign investors, import protection and export promotion, and exchange-rate management. These measures are expected to have catalyzing effects on the performance of economic zones over time. However, these prospects may be undermined by the underlying macroeconomic vulnerabilities of these economies. These may be due to (i) a legacy of complex institutional and industrial structures (extensive state participation in economic activity that may crowd out private participation);

(ii) relatively small size resulting in uneven distribution of population; (iii) abundance of natural resources with competitive and comparative advantages but mainly in the mining products; and (iv) landlocked geography that leads to higher trade and transport costs.

There have been consistent efforts to turn some of these vulnerabilities into opportunities through regional cooperation and international agreements. The CAREC Program, for instance, has invested heavily in transport infrastructure to integrate the Central Asian countries regionally and with global markets. The development of regional infrastructure is supported by various initiatives to promote trade, helping them reach out to global markets. Further, the bilateral relations at the political level have significantly improved and regional cooperation is seen as critical to the successful implementation of the national development plans. There has already been a surge in border cooperation to promote connectivity and intraregional trade within the STKEC region. In addition, all three countries are participating in regional groupings, including the CIS and the CIS Free Trade Area. These regional agreements can be the building blocks in deepening regional cooperation. Finally, there is a political momentum for increased international cooperation, which is crucial for promoting trade and investment.

Planned and/or proposed actions. The following actions are planned or proposed to develop SEZs and industrial zones in the STKEC region:

(i) **Align the special economic zones with economic realities.**
  (a) Design an SEZ policy that will address the most challenging institutional constraints that inhibit private investment.
  (b) Introduce deeper economic reforms with greater devolution of powers to regional and SEZ authorities in decision-making related to industrial zones and SEZs.
  (c) Align SEZs with the competitive advantages of the economy and allow a wider range of economic activities within SEZs (that are not prohibited by law in the country).

(ii) **Strengthen nonmanufacturing special economic zones**. Industrial zones and SEZs can help unlock the potential of certain sectors in countries where these have natural advantages for catalyzing the process of economic growth.
  (a) **Agro-industrial zones.** While all three countries have advantages in agricultural production, productivity remains rather low. Agro-industrial zones can focus on promoting agricultural productivity, production, and agriculture-based industrialization using both backward (implements and machines, and other materials) and forward linkages (agro and food processing).
  (b) **Logistics parks.** Countries that depend on commodity trade consisting of agricultural and mining products are often vulnerable to high logistics costs due to landlocked geography and warehousing issues. Infrastructure and markets are not well suited to deal with larger quantities of perishable products, and farmers lack the capacity to store or transport such products. Logistics centers offer opportunities for aggregation, packaging, and processing. Similarly, the transport logistics of mining products is a challenge due to the geographic isolation of many operations, and heavy weight and large size of the products. Logistics zones in the STKEC region can significantly reduce logistics costs by offering effective solutions and generating greater employment.

(iii) **Develop tourism zones.** The region has an enormous tourism potential. Awarding an SEZ status to geographically delineated areas can have a catalyzing effect on tourism in the region by standardizing and improving the services.

(iv) **Improve the attractiveness of special economic zones and industrial zones** by offering the following:
  (a) efficient and simplified institutional structure;
  (b) effective single window clearances;
  (c) stability in rules and regulations;

(d) world class infrastructure, testing and certification facilities, and efficient administrative services; and

(e) skills development and training for the labor force.

Important lessons may be drawn from the experiences of successful countries like Bangladesh, the PRC, the United Arab Emirates (particularly Dubai), Jordan, the Republic of Korea, and the Philippines, among others.

(v) **Promote domestic capacities through backward linkages.** The following can be undertaken:

(a) Build the capacity of domestic enterprises in the industrial zones by integrating them with those in SEZs.

(b) Complement infrastructure development with measures to promote human capital, product markets, financial systems, and innovations.

(vi) **Promote regional value chains** by undertaking the following:

(a) Identify the key sectors where regional value chains can flourish, based on regional comparative advantages (agro processing, metallurgy, machinery and equipment, chemical and petrochemicals).

(b) Identify the value chains to focus on in the selected sectors.

(c) Plan an appropriate strategy to harmonize the standards and regulations in the selected sectors, SEZs and regulations, and fiscal incentives.

(d) Strengthen domestic capabilities in participating and managing the chains through joint projects.

(e) Enhance the functionality of the product markets.

(vii) **Develop a sound implementation strategy** by

(a) employing a communication strategy with stakeholders and using dialogue for feedback and inputs to engage them in decision-making;

(b) allowing operational autonomy to zone management authorities on infrastructure development, services provided to tenants, and entry of residents, among others;

(c) developing human resource through training programs for the implementing personnel;

(d) imposing accountability and offering incentives to ensure commitment;

(e) exercising a macro management of the economy; and most importantly,

(f) harnessing engagements with regional and international cooperation for creating an environment where trade and investment can grow exponentially to enhance the effectiveness of SEZs.

(viii) **Establish a transparent monitoring and evaluation framework.** A clear framework for monitoring and evaluation (M&E) is essential to gauge the impact and success of the program in terms of the expected objectives and outcomes of the zone programs. There are global best practices that may be considered in designing the M&E framework. Maintaining systematic data on performance indicators is the first crucial step in this direction.

5 Expected Results

The development of the STKEC by implementing this road map is expected to have considerable positive effects. It will transform the STKEC region into a highly integrated and dynamic economic region characterized by the following:

(i)   Close economic cooperation among the Kazakh, Tajik, and Uzbek parts of the corridor in many areas, including transport and trade facilitation, agricultural research and development (R&D), plant and animal health protection, and tourism development.

(ii)   Superior transport connectivity within the region, among the STKEC countries, and with the rest of the world.

(iii)   Seamless movement of vehicles, goods, and people across borders within the region.

(iv)   Rapid technological progress and high productivity, especially along agricultural value chains.

(v)   Higher density of economic activity and robust economic growth, with convergence of living standards in various parts of the region.

(vi)   Extensive trade and investment flows among the Kazakh, Tajik, and Uzbek parts of the region.

(vii)   High levels of trade with the rest of the world, with large volumes of exports in horticulture goods, including organic produce, to European, Middle Eastern, and East Asian countries.

(viii) A vibrant tourism industry and large numbers of international tourist arrivals.

(ix)   Larger shares of manufactures and services, such as processed food products, and transport and tourism-related services, in exports.

Millions of people can benefit from the development of the STKEC. The number of people residing in the STKEC region is projected to increase from 11.1 million at the end of 2018 to 13.2 million by the end of 2030. With faster urbanization, the share of urban population in the STKEC region is forecast to rise from 54.2% at the end of 2018 to 59.1% by the end of 2030 (Table 20).

Table 20: Population of STKEC Region, 2018, 2025, and 2030 (by end of the year)

Population	2018 Actual	2025 Projection	2030 Projection
Total population (million)	11.1	12.3	13.2
Urban population (% of total population)	54.2	56.7	59.1
Rural population (% of total population)	45.8	43.3	40.9

STKEC = Shymkent–Tashkent–Khujand Economic Corridor.

Sources: Governments of Kazakhstan, Tajikistan, and Uzbekistan; and Asian Development Bank estimates.

Border crossing. As a result of modernizing the BCPs and border management, crossing borders between Turkestan and Tashkent oblasts and between Tashkent and Sugd oblasts will become much cheaper and faster (Table 21).

Table 21: Average Cost and Average Time Needed for Clearing Selected STKEC Border Crossing Points for Freight Traffic, 2019, 2025, and 2030

	Cost of Border Crossing ($)			Time Needed for Border Crossing (number of hours)		
	2019	2025	2030	2019	2025	2030
Border Crossing	Actual	Targets[a]	Targets[a]	Actual	Targets[a]	Targets[a]
Konysbayev–Yallama BCP	>100	80	40	>20	4	1
Oybek–Fotehobod BCP	>300[b]	200[b]	150[b]	>10	3	1
Saryagash–Keles BCP	>200	100	50	>10	5	2

BCPs = border crossing points, STKEC = Shymkent–Tashkent–Khujand Economic Corridor.

[a] The targets are preliminary. They will be revised, as appropriate, when there is more certainty about the medium- to long-term consequences of the coronavirus disease (COVID-19) pandemic for economic activity in the STKEC region.

[b] For trucks with a total load of more than 20 metric tons.

Sources: Central Asia Regional Economic Cooperation Corridor Performance Measurement and Monitoring dataset; and Asian Development Bank estimates.

Merchandise trade. Merchandise trade among the Kazakh, Uzbek, and Tajik parts of the region will rise from $341 million in 2018 to $1.6 billion in 2030 (Table 22). Transit trade with non-STKEC countries and the non-STKEC parts of the STKEC countries passing through the STKEC region will increase from $20.5 billion–$25.5 billion in 2018 to $38.0 billion in 2030.

Table 22: Intraregional Merchandise Trade in STKEC Region, 2018, 2025, and 2030
($ million)

Exporter	Importer	2018 Actual	2025 Targets[a]	2030 Targets[a]
Shymkent and Turkestan oblast	Sugd oblast	14	50	110
Shymkent and Turkestan oblast	Tashkent city and Tashkent oblast	136	320	660
Sugd oblast	Shymkent city and Turkestan oblast	1	20	60
Sugd oblast	Tashkent city and Tashkent oblast	78	140	220
Tashkent city and Tashkent oblast	Shymkent city and Turkestan oblast	76	200	450
Tashkent city and Tashkent oblast	Sugd oblast	36	60	80
Total		**341**	**790**	**1,580**

STKEC = Shymkent–Tashkent–Khujand Economic Corridor.

[a] The targets are preliminary. They will be revised, as appropriate, when there is more certainty about the medium- to long-term consequences of the coronavirus disease (COVID-19) pandemic for economic activity in the STKEC region.

Sources: Governments of Kazakhstan, Uzbekistan, and Tajikistan; and Asian Development Bank estimates.

Tourism. Over the medium to long term, the number of international visitor arrivals in the STKEC region will increase substantially (Table 23). There will be increases in intraregional tourism, of tourist arrivals from parts of the STKEC countries outside the region, and of international tourists who visit more than one STKEC country.

Table 23: Shymkent and Tashkent Cities and Turkestan and Tashkent Oblasts—International Visitor Arrivals, 2018, 2025, and 2030
('000)

	2018 Estimates	2025 Targets[a]	2030 Targets[a]
Shymkent city	178	500	1,000
Turkestan region	1,532	2,000	2,500
Tashkent city and Tashkent region	5,000	8,100	10,000
From Kazakhstan	2,200	2,600	3,000
From Tajikistan	1,000	1,500	2,000
From other countries	1,800	4,000	5,000
Of which: Tourists who visited or will visit more than one STKEC country	200	1,000	2,000

STKEC = Shymkent–Tashkent–Khujand Economic Corridor.

[a] The targets are preliminary. They will be revised, as appropriate, when there is more certainty about the medium- to long-term consequences of the coronavirus disease (COVID-19) pandemic for economic activity in the STKEC region.

Sources: Governments of Kazakhstan and Uzbekistan; and Asian Development Bank estimates.

Growth of gross regional product. The development of the STKEC will contribute to the acceleration of gross regional product (GRP) growth of Shymkent and Tashkent cities and Turkestan, Tashkent, and Sugd oblasts (Table 24).

Table 24: Average Annual Growth Rate of Gross Regional Product of Shymkent and Tashkent Cities and Turkestan, Tashkent, and Sugd Oblasts, Selected Periods
(%)

	2014–2018 Actual	2021–2025 Targets[a]	2026–2030 Targets[a]
Shymkent city and Turkestan oblast	9.8[b]	10.5	11.0
Tashkent city	10.6	11.0	11.5
Tashkent oblast	4.9	6.0	8.0
Sugd oblast	10.9	11.0	12.0

[a] The targets are preliminary. They will be revised, as appropriate, when there is more certainty about the medium- to long-term consequences of the coronavirus disease (COVID-19) pandemic for economic activity in the Shymkent–Tashkent–Khujand Economic Corridor region.

[b] The average annual growth rate of real growth regional product of former South–Kazakhstan oblast during 2014–2017.

Sources: Governments of Kazakhstan, Tajikistan, and Uzbekistan; International Monetary Fund; and Asian Development Bank estimates.

Sector composition of gross regional product. The share of manufacturing and/or service sectors in GRP will increase due to the relatively faster growth of these sectors (Table 25).

Table 25: Share of Selected Sectors in Gross Regional Product of Shymkent and Tashkent Cities and Turkestan, Tashkent, and Sugd Oblasts, 2018, 2025, and 2030
(%)

	2018 Actual	2025 Targets[a]	2030 Targets[a]
Shymkent city			
Manufacturing	22.6	24	25
Services	61.0	60	60
Turkestan oblast			
Manufacturing	9.9	12	14
Services	48.5	50	50
Tashkent city			
Services	50.0	53	55
Tashkent oblast			
Services	22.3	25	28
Sugd oblast			
Manufacturing	14.1	16	18
Services	40.9	43	45

[a] The targets are preliminary. They will be revised, as appropriate, when there is more certainty about the medium-term consequences of the coronavirus disease (COVID-19) pandemic for economic activity in the Shymkent–Tashkent–Khujand Economic Corridor region.

Sources: Governments of Kazakhstan, Tajikistan, and Uzbekistan; International Monetary Fund; and Asian Development Bank estimates.

Implications for Central Asia. The development of the STKEC will benefit not only the STKEC region but also the rest of Central Asia. It will further improve the relations among the STKEC countries, promote sustainable economic growth and shared prosperity in Central Asia, and enhance stability and security in the region. In particular, the development of the STKEC will help STKEC countries diversify the composition of their exports away from primary commodities and toward manufactured goods and services and reduce their vulnerability to the volatility of world commodity prices.

6 Implementation Arrangements

Taking into account the international experience in transnational economic corridor (TNEC) development—the Almaty–Bishkek Economic Corridor (ABEC) in particular—it is proposed that an STKEC Steering Committee, STKEC Thematic Working Groups (TWGs), and an STKEC Secretariat be established to implement this road map. The Steering Committee will consist of the CAREC National Focal Points for the STKEC countries; deputy mayors of the Shymkent, Tashkent, and Khujand cities; and deputy governors of the Turkestan, Tashkent, and Sugd oblasts. The committee will oversee the overall progress of the STKEC development and review the proposals made by the STKEC TWGs. It will report to the bilateral Intergovernmental Commissions of the STKEC countries.

A TWG will be established for each of the thematic focus areas of STKEC development. The TWGs will consist of representatives of central and local government agencies and the business communities of the three countries. They will propose actions and projects aimed at developing the STKEC and help resolve issues in the implementation of approved actions and projects. They will report to the Steering Committee.

The secretariat will consist of representatives from focal agencies of the STKEC countries. It will monitor progress in the STKEC development, prepare periodic progress reports, and organize meetings for the Steering Committee and the TWGs. ADB will support the STKEC Secretariat. The STKEC bodies will closely coordinate their work with CAREC bodies (Figure 9).

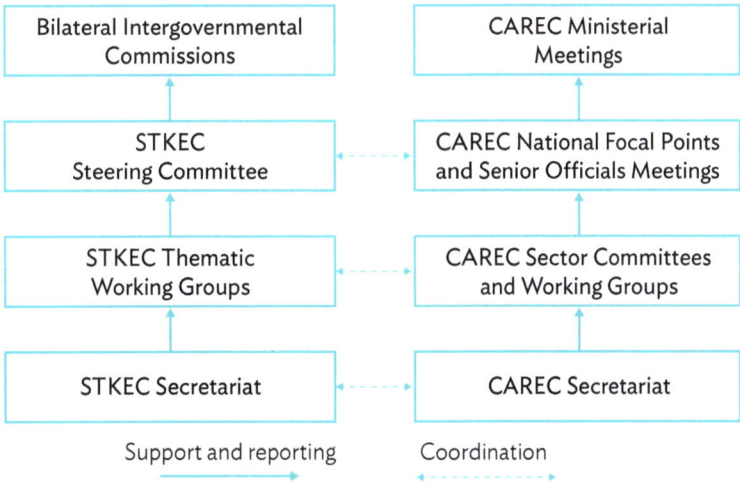

Figure 9: Institutional Setup for STKEC Development

CAREC = Central Asia Regional Economic Cooperation, STKEC = Shymkent–Tashkent–Khujand Economic Corridor.
Source: Asian Development Bank.

The implementation of the road map will be periodically evaluated. The road map will be revised or updated as needed.

The development of the STKEC will be project-driven. TA and investment projects will be implemented for each of the thematic focus areas to foster STKEC development. A list of possible projects that ADB and other development partners can potentially support is presented in the Appendix.

Appendix: Possible Projects

Thematic Focus Area	Project Scope	Project Type
Improvement of transport connectivity	Construction of a Saryagash bypass road in Turkestan oblast, construction of a Chirchik ring road in Tashkent oblast, and rehabilitation of the Khujand–Asht road in Sugd oblast.	Public investment projects, some of which may involve PPPs
	Strengthening of road operation and maintenance in STKEC countries—by introducing performance-based contracts and intelligent transport systems, including automated weigh-in-motion systems.	Public investment and regional TA projects
	Modernization of railway transport in STKEC countries—through the electrification of railways in the STKEC region and introduction of modern information and communication technologies, such as RFID technology.	Public investment and regional TA project
Improvement of transport connectivity and development of regional tourism	Rehabilitation of secondary and tertiary roads to enable access to tourism sites in the STKEC region.	Public investment projects
	Construction of a Turkestan–Shymkent–Tashkent high-speed railway.	Public investment project
Improvement of transport connectivity and development of SEZs and industrial zones	Construction of a railway extension that will connect the railway network in the southern part of Sugd oblast with the northern part of the oblast (where the Sugd free economic zone is located).	Public investment project
Modernization of BCPs and border management	Modernization of infrastructure, equipment, and procedures at selected STKEC BCPs (e.g., the Oybek–Fotehobod BCP).	Public investment and TA projects
	Introduction of the eTIR system, ATA carnet system, and CATS/ICE in STKEC countries.	Regional TA projects
	Conduct of the Time Release Studies covering the main STKEC BCPs.	Regional TA project

continued on next page

continued Possible Projects

Thematic Focus Area	Project Scope	Project Type
Development of horticulture value chains	Rehabilitation and upgrade of irrigation infrastructure (e.g., in Asht and Match districts of Sugd oblast) and expansion of the use of water-saving technologies (such as drip irrigation) in the STKEC region.	Public investment projects
	Strengthening of horticulture-related research and development, agricultural extension services, and marketing and export promotion; development and introduction of digital applications for farmers; and establishment of horticulture cooperatives and clusters and regional online marketplaces for farm inputs and agricultural goods (including fruits and vegetables).	Regional TA projects
	Establishment of a regional network of modern agro-logistics centers in the STKEC region.	Public investment and TA projects involving PPPs
	Assistance to horticulture cooperatives and clusters and agro-logistics centers so they could ensure food safety, produce or supply organic products, and obtain international food quality certificates.	Regional TA project
Modernization of SPS measures and development of food quality certification services	Modernization of food safety systems in STKEC countries by adopting farm-to-fork approach to food safety; conducting training programs in HACCP, GAP, GHP, ISO 22000 and other food safety standards; and enhancing competition in the market for food quality certification services.	Regional TA project
	Modernization of animal health protection in STKEC countries by introducing electronic veterinary certificates, establishing a regional animal identification and traceability system, and transitioning to risk-based veterinary control over international trade.	Public investment and TA project
	Modernization of plant protection in STKEC countries by introducing electronic phytosanitary certificates, strengthening the capacity of plant protection agencies for pest surveillance and pest risk analysis, and transitioning to a risk-based phytosanitary control over international trade.	Regional TA project
	Establishment of a network of SPS laboratories with ISO 17025:2017 international accreditation in the STKEC region.	Public investment and TA projects
Development of regional tourism	Support for revitalizing and development of the tourism industry in the STKEC region by developing and implementing enhanced health and safety standards and protocols; strengthening the capacity of central and local government agencies in charge of tourism development; providing support to the cross-border collaboration of government agencies and business communities in developing regional tourism; and establishing joint online tourism-related training programs.	Regional TA project
	Conduct of a feasibility study on the development of road and other infrastructure needed to connect recreational tourism sites in the eastern part of Turkestan oblast with those in the northern part of Tashkent oblast.	Regional TA project

continued on next page

continued Possible Projects

Thematic Focus Area	Project Scope	Project Type
Development of SEZs and industrial zones and development of horticulture value chains	Establishment of agro-industrial zones in Tashkent and Sugd oblasts.	Public investment and TA projects involving PPPs
Development of SEZs and industrial zones	Establishment of a transparent performance monitoring and evaluation systems for the SEZs and industrial zones in the STKEC countries.	Regional TA project
	Conduct of a feasibility study for the establishment of a cross-border trade center on the border between Turkestan and Tashkent oblasts.	Regional TA project

ATA = Admission Temporaire/Temporary Admission, BCPs = border crossing points, CATS/ICE = CAREC Advanced Transit System/Information Common Exchange, eTIR = electronic TIR, GAP = good agricultural practices, GHP = good hygiene practices, HACCP = Hazard Analysis and Critical Control Point, ISO = International Organization for Standardization, PPP = public–private partnerships, RFID = radio frequency identification, SEZs = special economic zones, SPS = sanitary and phytosanitary, STKEC = Shymkent–Tashkent–Khujand Economic Corridor, TA = technical assistance.

Source: Asian Development Bank.

www.ingramcontent.com/pod-product-compliance
Lightning Source LLC
Chambersburg PA
CBHW050050220326
41599CB00045B/7356